NEAR-SEX EXPERIENCES

A Woman In Crescendo, Aging with Bravado

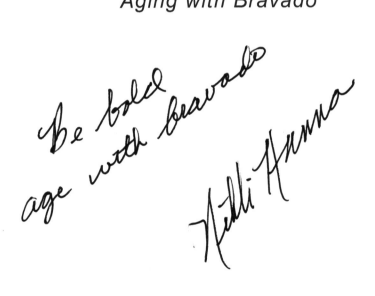

Be bold age with bravado

Nikki Hanna

N i k k i   H a n n a

Published by Patina Publishing
727 S. Norfolk Avenue
Tulsa, Oklahoma 74120
neqhanna@sbcglobal.net
www.nikkihanna.com

IBSN:978-0-9978141-2-5

Photography: Steven Michaels, Tulsa, Oklahoma
Cover Design: L1graphics
Artwork: Nan McDowell, Jenks, Oklahoma

Contributors: Lhonda Harris, Tom Bush,
Donna Parsons, Sallie Godwin,
Maxine Carlson,
Mikael Newman, Cynthia Vanderpool

Author's Note

I arranged for my photographer, Steven, to take a picture of me with a life-sized nutcracker to illustrate a playful example of a near-sex experience. We met at the location where this nutcracker served as a Christmas decoration. Steven noticed paint peeling in the area of the nutcracker's crotch. He asked if I had been practicing, which meant he grasped the concept of this book. In case you're wondering what a near-sex experience is, following is an example: When I suggest to male coffee buddies I'm wearing leather slacks so I smell like a new truck, they turn into something similar to outdoor tomcats, and their laughter hugs me. And that, my dear readers, is a near-sex experience.

Dedication

To Sam Elliott: A fabulous seventy-one-year-old masculine piece of bravado and sensitivity who enters a scene with a rakish swagger, causing the air around him to dissipate as he holds the universe together.

To the men I've loved: Because of them, when I'm asked to check a box for *sex* on forms, I draw my own box for *not pertinent*.

To my mixed salad of friends—my tribe: These people soften my world and offer up symphonies of advice, always issued with love, though sometimes misguided. After a breakup, one of them advised that if I wanted to get stalked, I should go to a furniture store or a car lot.

To Dad: Who gave me the courage to shed my dignity for the delight of humor and to value irreverence. A genius at finding the novelty in circumstances, he inspired in me an appreciation for the absurd and a flair for the cadence of swearing.

To my therapist: When I mucked around in a funk and bared my soul, she had the self-discipline to not say, "Well, that was weird."

Aging is where the dark and the light collide.
You can't eliminate the dark by ignoring it.
But you can shine in the glow of the light.

TABLE OF CONTENTS

POETRY

Introduction

It is a major challenge for a writer to get an agent interested in a book. So I was shocked when the mere mention of the title of this one prompted an agent to throw a business card at me and ask for the manuscript. In that moment I knew I was on to something.

The challenge became how to create an interior that measured up to that title. This proved more difficult than expected. Twice I gave up, but when I rallied, a saucy, amusing romp through the lives of older people evolved. This journey launched a diverse collection of vignettes in several genres—memoir, creative non-fiction, fiction, short story, and poetry—most peppered with humor. (In some cases, names were changed and liberties taken with facts to protect identities.)

Please forgive the serious expository speed bumps in the form of two meandering essays laden with haiku and academic impertinence. This deviation from the playful tone of the book reflects my lack of literary discipline. Also, a dash of snarky, inappropriate, unsophisticated, improper poetry that sucks delivers quirky interpretations and suggests the need for a pre-emptive apology. I include these divergent compositions because they are rich with lessons learned. And they blend easily into the cohesive whole of this book by virtue of the common thread of the aging experience.

In my mid-sixties, I learned aging is not so much about the body as it is about the mind. This perspective did not come easily. Ambushed by old age in my early sixties, I leaned into a gnawing depression. The rally from that low point was spectacular, and I wrote about it in *Red Heels and Smokin'—How I Got My Moxie Back.* Now I'm experiencing the remarkable residual effects of that recovery.

While peeling back layers of discontent during that transitional time, the subject of sex intruded. Its manifestation endures throughout life—ebbing and flowing until eventually acquiescing to reality. When men can only run to the end of the chain and bark, they still think and talk about sex. Women may move on from exotic sex to the basic starfish position, but their minds still rustle with erotic thoughts. Not to be underestimated, sex is about more than a physical encounter. Whether experienced or simply contemplated, it is a path to validation and to embracing the warmth of others.

Straining against the inevitable, men and women flirt and tease. As bodies morph, ladies hate their ugly clothes, squeeze into shape wear, and wonder, "Am I sexy yet?" Men settle into a blend of tentative lament and reluctant acceptance as robust experiences fade. These outcomes do not necessarily suggest malcontent. Real sex may lose its shine, but near-sex experiences tantalize like chocolate.

What is a near-sex experience? Does mooning qualify? Groping a life-sized nutcracker? Folding men's underwear warm from the dryer? Experiencing a senior sixty-nine by simultaneously rubbing each other's feet? A young help-desk genius asking if your cookies are activated? K-Y jelly on a thumb so it doesn't get stuck in a bowling ball? Amy Poehler described one on Saturday Night Live when she said, "I put my phone on vibrate, sit on it, and call myself over and over."

All of these do qualify, I suppose. Near-sex experiences reside in the minds of those experiencing them and in the margins of the real deal. They go to the heart of the connectedness everyone craves from cradle to grave. Such experiences are, by their nature, provocative. I can write about them now because I'm old and can therefore abandon propriety. I have no job, my children are grown, and my parents aren't here anymore. My apologies to Aunt Weezie, who is still here.

Women over fifty are the primary target audience for this book. My writing tends to take men to a level of confusion they've never before experienced since I am reckless with interpretations of their observations. This is because I don't understand men any better at seventy than I did at seventeen. While women read *Eat, Pray, Love*, men read *Drink, Party, Fuck*, a real book that proves my point.

Near Sex Experiences may not be as tantalizing as its title implies, but it does project a salty tone. If you are easily offended, this book is not for you. My girlfriends—whom no one would describe as uptight and proper—encourage me to be bold, so saucy repartee peppers this narrative.

My wish for you, dear reader, is that you find this unconventional conglomeration of references to the spicy side of aging entertaining. I hope the messages help you find your own sweet spot in the realm of life in spite of formidable challenges. I hope you are entertained and enlightened by lessons shared. And I hope you are inspired to orchestrate your own crazy-wonderful gift of legacy by how you age.

When it comes to aging, everyone is afraid on the inside. Gratefulness is the key to coping. Growing old is a blessing. It is the universe showing off, and it's time not everyone gets. If you are in the third trimester of life, this is your time, and it can be your best time.

*You know that look women get when they want to have sex? Me neither. . .*Steve Martin

Chapter 1

The Naked Cowboy

My life has come to this.

While attending a writers' conference in New York City, I came across The Naked Cowboy, a fixture in Times Square. He wasn't actually naked. His attire consisted of white briefs, a white cowboy hat, and white cowboy boots. Women stand in line to have their pictures taken with him and to cram money into his white guitar.

I typically find buffed-up men only marginally attractive, and when I see one, I'm not inclined to want to climb that tree. But I spotted the fellow when in a festive, touristy, New York frame of mind and that seemed like enough reason to have my picture taken with him.

As the photographer prepared to shoot, The Naked Cowboy instructed me to turn my back to the camera and put my hand on his butt. I did as instructed. And he put his hand on mine. As I looked back at the photographer for the shoot, this seductive cowboy in Jockey shorts nibbled on my neck—at which time I realized I wasn't dead yet.

Afterward, while shoving a five dollar bill into his guitar, I considered whether I had thoroughly abandoned all pretense of dignity. I wasn't sure what to do with the picture but finally settled on using it to impress my seventy-something-year-old girlfriends back in Oklahoma and to terrorize my children, which is always fun.

I texted them the picture. Although my children were aware I was in New York for a conference—one, no doubt, composed mostly of restrained, introverted writers—they also knew their mother sometimes did things she shouldn't. However, they did not expect a picture of Mom with a cowboy in Jockey shorts holding her butt, her holding his, and a caption that said, "I l-o-v-e New York."

My daughter texted back, "Don't call me if you get thrown into a New York City jail."

The message to my girlfriends said, "Another near-sex experience." They were appropriately impressed and gloriously jealous. That's when it occurred to me how often sexual innuendos pepper my life, even though I am old by any standard. I concluded: What a concept for a book.

Chapter 2

Mooning–A Near-Sex Experience?

You have to learn to get up from the table
when love is no longer being served. . .Nina Simone

After ten years, Brook's boyfriend left her for a woman thirty years her junior. As she and her friends entered a Holiday Inn in Florida, her anger showed. "My ultimate fantasy is that he dies, and I'm still the beneficiary on his life insurance."

"It's okay to be bitter for a while," Roxie, said, "but at some point you must move on. You don't want to be putting Round-Up on his grave someday."

Brook, a retired college professor, bounced along in round-toed Mary Janes, her skirt rustling around her ankles. Curly, auburn-tinged hair billowed poncho-like, making her look larger than she was. Buddha-inspired jewelry hinted at a search for serenity. Her appearance contrasted sharply with her friends, Roxie and DeeDee, who were decked out in coordinated resort wear. The two planned this trip to facilitate Brook's healing from the devastation of betrayal.

Roxie, a tough, no-nonsense gal whom friends labeled The Queen of Banter, did not hold back. "You know he possesses the sensitivity of a Somalian raider. Remember when you crawled catlike into bed in a teddy and he said, 'Can we lose the jumpsuit?'"

Brook laughed. "Yeah, I came in hot, and that happened."

"He has the intelligence of celery and the ambition of a sloth."

Brook chuckled. "Why don't you tell me what you really think?"

DeeDee interrupted. "Come on, girls. We've got to register." The ladies approached the registration desk, oblivious to the spring break fiasco taking place on the beach.

* * *

Jason, the youthful registration clerk, shifted nervously from foot to foot as he observed the ladies approach. They pushed along suitcases almost as big as they were and juggled citrus-colored sun hats, large purses, designer sunglasses, and souvenir bags from airport shops. These were, no doubt, well-travelled women accustomed to exclusive hotels that offer bellmen, chocolates on pillows at night, and safes in which to store jewelry.

Jason possessed a rare appreciation for older women. The ladies reminded him of his grandmother, whom he considered a freaking supernova. He greeted them with a genuine smile. DeeDee, who always made travel arrangements for their adventures, asked, "What's your name?"

"Jason."

"Well, Jason, These gals, Roxie and Brook, are in a foul mood, so let's you and I talk. How about an upgraded room?"

"Let's do it." He hustled to check them in while the lobby was in a rare interlude of calm. This could change at any moment. "I'm putting you in an end unit on the top floor."

"Nice," DeeDee responded. To Jason's surprise, Roxie performed a joyful hop completely out of character for an older woman and put her hand up to Brook for a high five. They missed each other's hands and tried unsuccessfully several more times to connect before transitioning into playful hitting. *Well, that's novel. I hope the old gals don't hurt themselves.*

Roxie continued badgering Brook, "What kind of idiot is a fan of Sharknado? The man's a dolt."

Brook's body stiffened. "Shut up."

"You shut up."

"No, you shut up."

"You S-H-U-T U-P."

"You both shut up," DeeDee interjected.

"Are you sisters?" Jason asked.

"No, and I don't know these people."

Brook resumed, "He did suck the life out of me. So why am I hurting?"

"Because you're an idiot."

"Why would you say such an awful thing?"

"I'm trying to be poetic."

Jason forced himself to focus. He put iridescent, rubber security bands on the ladies' wrists, which distracted them from the man-rage. Although puzzled by this novel twist, the girls considered the bands arm candy. "Makes me feel sporty," Roxie said. She struck a series of ridiculous Hans and Franz poses. Brook joined in.

Jason laughed. *Maybe their sense of humor will carry them through their stay.* "You're checked in," he said. "Would you like tickets for a free breakfast buffet?"

"Oh, yes," DeeDee responded.

Jason suggested another accommodation. "How about coupons for drinks at the Tiki bar?"

"Fabulous," said Roxie, who believed wine was a category in Maslow's hierarchy of needs. Once a well-traveled corporate attorney, Roxie was now retired and focused on pro bono human rights work. She missed expense reports and exclusive hotel lounges.

"Perhaps you'd like earplugs?" Jason asked.

"How nice." DeeDee found the novelty of earplugs perplexing but attributed the unconventional perk to her astute selection of an accommodating hotel.

"Have a nice stay. Let me know if you need anything." Jason smiled. He shook his head as he watched the ladies walk away, wrestling luggage, and all talking at the same time.

* * *

As they headed to the elevators, the ladies anticipated a fabulous Florida experience at what was apparently an exceptionally accommodating Holiday Inn. Rounding the corner to the elevators, they ran into a roped entrance and a security guard who demanded to see their wristbands. Sand grated on the soles of their designer shoes. Two cops, escorting cuffed, dejected-looking juveniles in swim trunks, maneuvered through the women and their substantial luggage.

Abrasive noises and bump and grind music blasted through doors down the hall leading to the beach. When elevator doors opened, screams and laughter exploded as young people poured out. Teenage boys in swim trunks so baggy they looked like skirts and nearly naked, oiled-up young girls boisterously refilled the elevators. DeeDee, who did fundraising for victims of human trafficking, was sensitive to the display. "These girls' mothers don't know their daughters are wearing bikinis that look like stripper pasties."

Roxie realized that to get to their room, the women had to go shoulder-to-shoulder with the feral children. She posted herself in front of an elevator door and shepherded her friends in. As the door closed, the women found themselves crushed by a swarm of wet, rowdy, sexed-up teens. The ladies' polished appearance and Rubenesque figures contrasted sharply with the other passengers. The novelty of this was not lost on the young.

"What college are you from?" a bikini-clad child chided.

Not grasping the sarcasm, DeeDee replied, "Oh, we're not students. We're here for a reunion with our groupies."

"You have groupies?" The uptick in the girl's voice reflected her surprise.

"Just two," DeeDee answered matter of factly, still unaware of the girl's teasing. She started to elaborate, but the youngster reached her floor. The remaining "children" showed no interest in anything except jovial banter and rubbing sunbaked bodies against one another.

A boy asked the girl pressing up against him, "Would you basically like to come to my room and like have a beer?"

Brook whispered in Roxie's ear, "California sissy speak does not wear well on a guy. And that girl's boobs are bigger than her head. She should not be in a bikini."

"I bet she has skills," Roxie whispered.

The door opened and four glassy-eyed boys pushed their way onto the elevator. One pressed against an oiled-up beauty and asked if she wanted to get pregnant.

The girl revealed a strong bullshit meter. "You're ugly."

"Not so."

"You want a second opinion?"

"Yeah."

"You're stupid, too." Laughter spilled into the hall as the elevator doors opened. When it arrived on the top floor, only the ladies and a couple of love birds were left and the hallway took on an air of relative calm. Brook and her friends rolled their suitcases down the hall. The room, though tinged with musty beach smells and air freshener, was pleasant enough. As Brook and Roxie unpacked, DeeDee opened the door to the balcony to survey the view. A roar too loud to be the ocean blasted into the room. "Come quick. You've got to see this."

Brook and Roxie hurried to the balcony to discover a wave of people up and down the beach moving rhythmically to bump and grind music and periodically howling in response to announcements from a deejay. Lights surrounding his music station pulsated so furiously they could trigger seizures. A crush of bodies circled the station and a Tiki bar. Entangled bodies, bobbing up and down with the waves, peppered the ocean. Braying youngsters gyrated on balconies.

Festive young men on the next balcony whooped and hollered. They toasted the ladies. One of them asked, "Wanna fuck?"

Not one to be intimidated by offensive propositions, Roxie yelled, "You'd be so in over your head you don't even know."

Brook asked DeeDee. "Holy crap. How did *this* happen?"

"I thought spring break would be over."

"Well, it's clearly not. How much Ambien did you bring?"

"Not enough."

The Breakup

This trip was planned on short notice when the girls got together at their hangout in Tulsa, Oklahoma, to commiserate with

Brook on her breakup. She had always been a confident, accomplished woman who once told her man, "If you find a better deal than the one you've got, you'd better take it." Ultimately, he did. The resulting betrayal left her unanchored. Bruised from crushing disappointment and tarnished romance, she had fallen into a gloomy state. Her girlfriends, desperate to save her, determined their groupie friends would be good medicine. It was time to round up the boys.

DeeDee, who was usually in charge of their travel plans, targeted Florida for the reunion. One of the groupies lived there and the beach environment would be soothing, or so she thought. Spring break was not on her radar when she booked the trip.

Brook wasn't the only one unlucky at love. DeeDee had her share of failed romances but remained resilient. She never gave up on finding the right man; however, she was not clamoring for a spot in someone else's life. Volunteer work, two cats, and taking care of her aging mother fulfilled her.

Roxie, on the other hand, was completely done—fried, cooked, burnt out. A tough old bird, she was never one to go gonzo on some guy when he displeased her. She just set him free. Somewhat of a man-magnet in spite of being in her sixties, she reacted sharply to propositions. When a man asked her out, she declined. When they asked why, she gave an honest answer. "I must protect you from yourself." If a determined fellow pursued the case further, she explained, "It's like this. If you expect a casserole, I'll tell you to talk to the casserole fairy."

Brook now carried the same baggage of bitterness as Roxie. She told her friends, "I've bounced too often between the extremes of manhood. Men either saw me as a Middle-Eastern sex slave or complained I made them feel inadequate."

Roxie responded, "That's because they were inadequate."

"It's a good thing you girls aren't bitter," DeeDee said, proud of her rare expression of sarcasm.

Brook defended her newly-found, negative position by revealing her vulnerability. "All I know is I don't have another breakup in me."

Roxie, who coped with aloneness by focusing on travel, three grandchildren, and a post retirement career of pro bono work, responded, "Yeah, what she said."

Brook continued, "If I'm done with love, I don't understand why my not-so-fine man is so hard to shake. I keep going over 'if only' propositions."

DeeDee comforted her friend with a rationalization. "Your torment is because of the ego-busting blow common among older women when a man leaves them for a younger one. You should get over that because you know he didn't move up with that one."

"Well, he clearly thinks he did. That grates on me. It's wounding. He traded me for a dollar store clerk with three kids, credit card debt, an unreliable car, and a flair for stick-on fingernails. I must be a sad, sorry piece of shit to lose my man to such a woman."

Roxie couldn't hold back. "You need to graciously give your ex to the less fortunate and ride that misery down, girlfriend.

And, one more thing, you are not depressed. You had simply taken up with an asshole. You need a distraction. Let's go to Florida."

The Groupies

The girls have been tight since bonding in graduate school. Together they raised children, earned degrees, and functioned for years as professional women in a wasteland devoid of female perspectives and lush with male egos. In that environment, they supported each other through the early career years and reveled in the accomplishments of later ones. Now they were retired.

Over the years, they met frequently for dalliances at their favorite after-work grill where they linked up with two single Tulsa businessmen. Conner, known for his intuitive interpretations of human behavior, and Steven, whose excessive energy level inspired the nickname Sparky, had become the girls' confidantes and consultants. The men were much younger, but both they and the girls were proficient at compartmentalizing members of the opposite sex into the friend zone. As the dynamics of the group evolved, all five became tight.

The men came up with their label as groupies. Suffering from the inconvenience of being male feminists, they related instantly to the girls' career-oriented personas and championed them enthusiastically. The girls' exceptional knack for matching the groupies in the area of irreverence entertained the guys and contributed to the lasting bond. After-work socials became the highlight of their days.

Sparky, a fellow not naturally proficient at editing his remarks, somehow managed enough self-discipline to succeed as a corporate sales executive. In other settings, he was a bit of a mess. Roxie described him this way: "He's not the kind of guy you want to introduce to your evangelistic mother." Because of their own tendency toward irreverence, the girls tolerated his vulgarities and brash enthusiasm. His sharp mind, zest for life, and good heart made up for shortcomings. When he got too outrageous and unleashed pent-up crazy, DeeDee's ultra-sensitive nature kicked in, and she reminded her friends that everyone is deserving of God's grace.

Although a fastidious dresser with a meticulously detailed car, Sparky was otherwise a slob—a guy who cleaned his beige house with a leaf blower once a year whether it needed it or not. Roxie described it as the kind of place you wake up in after being slipped a mickey. DeeDee was right about his heart. To make up for his own difficult childhood, Sparky coached basketball for an organization that redeemed wayward teens. These youthful admirers occupied much of his time and energy, and he spent little time at home.

Sparky playfully and relentlessly propositioned the girls. At the height of his impertinence, he assured a resistant Roxie he would be in and out quickly and she wouldn't even notice. "You're going to admit that?" she asked. In retaliation, she called him *Lightning*, a label his quirky persona welcomed.

The two groupies did not bond tightly with each other as men often do. Instead, they nestled into a state of easy coexistence. Conner considered Sparky a hopeless candidate for social reconstruction and disapproved of his uncouth repartee. Sparky ribbed Conner for being staid, for playing "Solitaire" manually with cards, and for possessing an iPhone four generations old.

Both were good-looking fellows, and over the years they often served as classy dates for the girls. However, as armchair capitalists, their enthusiasm for advising the women on relationship issues were often problematic. The male perspective was generally helpful, but they applied business principles to every situation, including romance. This created problems.

To determine whether one of the women should date a guy, the boys performed a *business analysis worthiness test*. This began with a pro forma projection on the prospects of a viable relationship. Data was gathered and analyzed, often on a napkin. Pros and cons were listed, return on investment calculated, opportunity costs considered, threats identified, competition examined, and optimal outcomes explored. After a breakup, a *residual value analysis* identified lessons learned. When Roxie dated a cowboy, the boys suggested a *contingency plan*. These business concepts explained why the women and their groupies rarely successfully dated anyone.

Their lives braided together over time and withstood the challenges of change. Conner married Allie, who somehow managed to pass the *business analysis worthiness test*, and moved to Florida.

Sparky received a promotion and transferred to Dallas. Brook retired from her professorship, moved to Colorado, and dedicated her time to writing books and babysitting grandchildren. After retirement, DeeDee became active in civic activities and devoted considerable time to caring for her aging mother. Roxie traveled extensively with *pro bono* work. The group's routine after-work gatherings transitioned into a mode of occasional reunions.

The Reunion

After the first night of surviving spring break hell, the girls headed to Conner and Allie's house, a brightly painted beach house softened with flora. Colorful painted rocking chairs, a porch swing, and potted plants adorned the front porch. Sparky was staying there. "I don't think I've ever been around Sparky when I didn't have a near-sex experience," Brook noted.

"I wonder if he really ever gets any. God knows he tries," DeeDee said.

"Oh, I'm sure he does. I mean, just look at those luscious baby blue, Paul Newman eyes and that great bod. He is fine. And no one is more fun. Unfortunately, he has the energy of a frantic Yorkie. And. . .and. . .and. . .Oh, hell. He's an obscenely hilarious nut job most of the time."

"What's he doing in Dallas these days?" DeeDee asked.

"Still working, and he coaches basketball at a boys' club."

"See, he's a good guy."

"Yeah, he's just a tad cray-cray."

When they arrived at Conner's place, Sparky ribbed Roxie, who had gained weight, "You look sturdy."

She responded, "You're an arrogant, weapons-grade asshole."

"Hey, I'm not arrogant."

The two hugged.

He gave a special hug to Brook as he lifted her off the ground and spun her around. "I've missed you."

"I've missed you, too, Sparky."

Connor swept Brook into a bear hug and then, with his hands on her shoulders, looked her in the eyes. "You are special. A man must earn you, you know."

Brook responded, "Now, tell me I'm pretty."

Conner's wife, Allie, gave Brook an extra squeeze and patted her on the back. As the newest member of the group, she had found her place. She accepted Conner's groupie role and generously shared him with the other women in his life.

Sparky asked Brook if he could be a character in the book she was writing. She responded, "Sure, I'll call you Lightning and bludgeon you to death in the first chapter while you are sleeping on a blowup doll." Sparky liked the idea.

Conner wanted in on the action. "What about me?"

"I need a good redneck, macho character. I'll call you Shithead. You'll drive around in a jacked-up truck, hunt Bambi, and wear pointy-toed, roach-killer boots with metal tips."

"Can I have a wo-o-oman who is built to show?"

"No. You can have random hair growth and skin tags the size of gerbils."

"Let's go," said Roxie, "before someone names the gerbils."

The group boarded a minivan DeeDee rented so everyone could ride in one vehicle. Since she tended to grip a wheel like a farmer plowing a field, came to complete stops before right-hand turns, and drove slow in fast lanes, Brook assumed the role of designated driver. She had no experience driving a van but managed to dodge spring breakers on scooters with finesse. "I feel rather macho in this massive vehicle," she bragged.

"You should feel like a soccer mom," Roxie responded, "or a UPS deliveryman."

"You look good driving," DeeDee interjected, hoping to forestall any negative joshing between her friends. Their conversations sometimes deteriorated into abrasiveness. Brook and Roxie were strong-willed, competitive women whose sarcastic humor often took on the tone of coarse barbs. Conner, full of positive juju, said, "Brook, you are a delicate feminine flower whose driving doesn't suck."

The day didn't go well. While stopped in beach-road traffic, an old primer-painted car crossed the center line. Brook groaned, "No-o-o-o" as the clunker ground into the van's front fender. She spewed swear words in a cadence that would have made her father proud. Roxie dialed the police. DeeDee dug in her purse for Xanax. Sparky regretted quitting smoking. Conner considered his next move.

A bent-over old geezer with a Civil War General's beard and pant legs tucked into well-worn boots exited his clunker to survey the damage. Feathers dangled from the back of his beat-up alligator hat. He loped like a man moseying out to his front porch to lounge on a Herculon upholstered chair and take a gander at the sunset while communing with hound dogs. Brook froze behind the wheel, so Conner exited the van to talk to the perpetrator.

Roxie griped, "He looks like one of those intellectually bankrupt rednecks who catches catfish with his hands."

DeeDee washed a pill down with water. "He's got a swagger that's kinda cute."

"Are you kidding? That's a stagger. He walks like a squirrel drunk on fermented berries."

Conner, always the reconciliatory force and a man who remains calm in times of chaos, initiated a friendly conversation with Mooney. A pathetic old fellow who smelled of alcohol, he explained his dilemma this way: "I drived down from Alabama to gits a tattoo. My shirt was a itchin' it, sos I's lookin' fer a t-shirt place. Den, dag nabbit, dis happened."

Brook knew the odds of Mooney having insurance was as likely as Sparky remembering to take his attention deficit medication that morning. Sparky fidgeted so frantically next to Conner that he looked like a robot disco dancer juiced up on meth.

One Mississippi, two Mississippi, three Mississippi, Hokey Pokey, marshmallows, touchdown, unicorns, polygamy, jigger of salt. What role do chiggers play in the scheme of nature?

"I paid $200 for dat dar car," Mooney said to the investigating policeman.

Without looking up from an in-process ticket, the officer responded, "It's probably worth $20 now."

As the officer let a wobbly Mooney off with just a ticket, probably because of Conner's influence, DeeDee said, "The poor old fellow. I'm glad he didn't get arrested."

Sparky bent the fender of the van out so it no longer rubbed against the tire. Back on the road, Brook apologized to the group for her swearing rant. Conner eased her remorse by comparing her expletives to a lyrical George Carlin routine.

She nursed the van to Conner's house where they picked up his car so he could follow them to the airport rental car lot in case there was trouble. Sparky rode with Conner. On the freeway, the guys pulled up beside the van and Sparky mooned the ladies out of the passenger window.

Brook laughed so hysterically she could hardly drive. "I'm in pain here."

"Is it okay to wet your pants in a rental car?" Roxie asked.

"That man needs therapy—a serious treatment plan."

In the rental car parking lot, DeeDee advised Sparky he had pimples on his butt. This shocked him, especially coming from DeeDee, who was not one to kid around. He denied it. She held her position.

At the airport rental car counter, DeeDee rented a fresh vehicle while Sparky propositioned Roxie. An expert at talking smack, she matched him, "That's equivalent to a naked person offering me a shirt."

"Now, that's a false equivalency," Sparky responded.

"You are a crime against humanity, Lightning. Did you take your meds today?" Sparky patted his pockets, produced a pill, and wandered off, looking for a drinking fountain.

The girls were soon headed to Conner's house in a different van. They passed Conner and Sparky on the highway. Sparky waved enthusiastically. The girls considered a payback for the mooning. Brook suggested DeeDee lift her shirt and plaster her boobs up against the window. In a less festive situation, the idea would have offended DeeDee, but she was still pumped from getting Sparky's goat with her pimple declaration.

"Do it," Roxie said. "It'll be a hoot. People will be tweeting about it off the coast of Angola." Conner pulled away, and the prospect of flashing boobs fell off the agenda. Roxie was disappointed, DeeDee relieved.

The Medicine

Aspirations for touring faded, so the group settled into the comfort of Conner's beach house. Allie fed them a meal Conner described as Mediterranean/Cuban fusion. They drank wine and reminisced. Roxie gave her signature toast, "To friends. May we never disagree. If we do, fuck you, here's to me."

As they lingered around the dining room table, Conner zeroed in on Brook, "How are you doing, girl?"

Roxie answered for her, "She thinks she's a sad, sorry piece of shit for losing her man to THAT woman."

"You are not a sad, sorry, piece of shit," DeeDee said.

"I'd fuck you," Sparky interjected.

"When will your pill kick in?" Roxie asked. "Perhaps you need another one."

Conner persisted. "You know you weren't happy."

Brook nodded. Tears formed in her eyes. "That's what puzzles me. How can I hurt so when he had changed so much that today I wouldn't even notice him? And why am I so devastated when I'm actually glad he's out of my life? Ego, I guess. The humiliation is epic. I'd feel better if he'd left me for a beautiful, ravishing woman. . . . No. I wouldn't. . . ." The tears were really flowing now. "I'm broken. I wish there was some medicine for that. I just want the hurting to stop." She put her head in her hands and sobbed. No words were spoken for what seemed like a long time. Awkward looks ping-ponged around the room. Allie rounded up a box of tissue. Sparky squirmed in his chair, his mind bouncing as if he were on a trampoline.

Conner reached over and cupped Brook's hands in his. "I'm sorry you are in this situation. No one deserves that. You know, love is all about how a person makes you feel. How did he make you feel?"

"Like I was an irritant. Oh, my god, how sad is that? I stayed and let him do that to me."

"How do you think you made him feel?"

"Like he was inadequate."

"He was inadequate," Roxie said. DeeDee nudged her.

"I wish I could be like Roxie and hate men," Brook said.

Roxie puffed up, "I don't hate men."

DeeDee knew when to step in. "She doesn't hate men. She just doesn't want one."

Brook continued, "Just when I think I'm better, a trigger is tripped and I shatter like glass. I need the hurting to stop."

"The medicine is yours, you know," Connor said. "You have more power than you realize. You just need some healing time. In about six months, you're going to emerge from this like a butterfly coming out of a cocoon. It's going to be grand. I can't wait to see it. Let's book our next reunion right now."

The girls pulled up calendars on phones. Sparky patted his pockets and darted around the room looking for his. Conner got up to get his and kissed Brook on the head in the process. Not to be outdone, Sparky said, "Hey, keep your hands off my woman." He strutted over and kissed Brook hard and long on the lips. Everyone cheered as Brook's whole body went limp. When he let go, she slid down to the floor laughing.

Sparky ran around the room pumping his fists in the air while humming Rocky's theme song.

Butterfly Power

The girls eventually headed back to spring break hell with thoughts of doses of Ambien while Sparky checked out his butt in a mirror. Once there, the Tiki bar called to them, and they dug free drink coupons out of purses. There was no avoiding the spring break hullabaloo, so they dove into the mix, choosing a table away from the balconies—lest a drunken child fall from above. Breathing in sweet smoke billowing over from a neighboring table, they sipped drinks with umbrellas in them.

Brook said, "I believe I've had two near-sex experiences today, if mooning is classified as one. That kiss sure was."

DeeDee rolled her eyes. "Mooning is inappropriate social behavior, and we should never speak of it again."

"You are joking, right? I've never been mooned before. It was like foreplay. I can't let go of that. I mean, it was a defining moment. And that kiss . . . I love me some Sparky." The girls laughed louder than the festive children surrounding them, who, no doubt, thought older people should not have more fun than they do.

"I think we're getting a gray-contact high from all the secondary smoke wafting over here. Any minute now, we'll be munching on the best celery ever. Did you know you cannot work a jigsaw puzzle if you're high?" Brook asked.

"Why not?"

"Each piece holds so much fascination that you hold it up to the light and go, 'W-o-w.' You can stare at it for hours."

Roxie responded, "How do you know that?" To keep the positive momentum going, she asked Brook, "What would make you feel better?"

"A Jaguar. . . . Actually, I want a new boyfriend."

"In that case, what color Jaguar do you want?"

"The hell with cars. I'm in a Bee Gees frame of mind. I want music, something besides this pounding noise."

"Good luck with that," Roxie responded. "I'm in an Audrey Hepburn frame of mind? Let's have ice cream."

"Audrey would have water and a crouton," Brook noted.

"Here's a good compromise. Let's have shots of Tequila Rose." And they did. Twice.

Flush with drink, DeeDee's speech took on a severe lisp as she recited a quote she thought would help cheer Brook up. "A hole in the heart isth what leths the light in."

Brook and Roxie stared at each other briefly and then responded simultaneously, "S-H-U-T T-H-E F-U-C-K U-P." DeeDee embraced the intended humor. Their robust laughter filled the air as even more sweet smoke curled over from the neighboring table. The ladies breathed deeply and high-fived each other in a round-table fashion, purposely missing each others' hands. As their actions progressed into a slapping match, mystified spring breakers looked on.

"Isthn't it inthereshting thath we are old, and we're sthill having tho much fun?" DeeDee asked.

"Yeah. I'm so happy I could wash dishes," Brook said.

* * *

The next morning the women mucked around in makeup and applied products designed to tame savage hair ballooning from humidity. DeeDee laid out a white lacy top reminiscent of the doilies Grandmas used to put on furniture, which caused Roxie to suggest she set a lamp on it.

"I didn't sleep well," Brook said. "I dreamed my date showed up in an NRA t-shirt."

DeeDee, who had taken two doses of Ambien said, "I dreamed I had insomnia." Roxie instructed her to let the boys and Allie know when they would arrive at Connor's place. DeeDee responded, "You are not the boss of me," before texting Sparky to advise him she would text him when they left the hotel. Auto correct changed the message to, "I will sex you when we leave the hotel." He responded, "Hot damn, girlfriend."

As Brook braided her mushrooming hair, she announced, "I think I'll go to Africa. Perhaps I can find a rich, white Republican on safari."

Roxie frowned. "Oh stop. You are not *that* desperate." To distract Brook from any more outrageous thoughts, she speculated on the first thing that came to mind. "I bet Weezer from Steel Magnolias could take out Saturday Night Live's Church Lady in a fight—if there were mud."

DeeDee stared at Roxie mystified, then looked at Brook, "Why don't you write about what happened, Brook?"

"I suspect I would come off as some kind of old Bridget Jones. Maybe I'll just write a poem."

Roxie interjected, "Whatever you do, just don't drunk dial or do drive bys. You haven't done either of those have you?"

"We-e-e-l-l-l. How else would I know the gal wears leather pants with a belt with handcuffs on it to the ballet?"

"Oh, my god. Drive bys are so-o-o-o juvenile. Why don't you do something sophisticated like sending him a bottle of Fat Bastard wine?"

"The guy is culturally marginal. I'd have to send him a six pack. I should just get over him. When this all started, I thought I would heal like a fury since I was glad to be rid of his gloomy self. So I don't understand why I'm so devastated. I'm feeling better, though. I want to reinvent myself—like a butterfly. This trip has been good for me. I'm excited about starting over. I'm so glad we did this."

"You do remember Sparky kissed you on the lips last night, don't you?" Roxie asked. "Did you get any tongue?"

DeeDee, determined to keep the conversation positive, offered a quote, "Happiness is where the light and the dark collide."

Roxie could not contain herself. "You are so-o-o deep."

Brook said, "My mouth tastes like copper pennies. Let's go have a free breakfast with the hungover children."

While waiting to be seated for breakfast, the ladies chatted with two young girls, the only children up early. One sported green hair reminiscent of a Muppet. Proud of her ability to overlook the bizarre hair and an unfortunate tattoo, DeeDee complimented her on her funky sunglasses and inquired about the girl's college major, which turned out to be finance. "Good choice," she said.

The ladies ate a free breakfast buffet and drank coffee so bad Brook described it as a crime against society. To ease her disappointment, she devoured a pile of grief bacon. DeeDee, who had an adversarial relationship with food, chomped down on a frosted donut and rationalized, "My extra weight makes my feet hurt, but it does make it harder for someone to abduct me."

"How much are you trying to lose?" Brook asked.

"Just twenty pounds. I've got twenty-five to go."

A group of messed-up, unsteady spring breakers entered the dining room. "Did you notice the kids on the elevator smelled like funky cantaloupe—my apologies to cantaloupes."

"It's hypocritical to make fun of them when people our age engage in mooning on the highway," DeeDee suggested.

"Mooning is different," Brook maintained. "It is only a near-sex experience. Who knows what those kids are doing?" Brook vowed to threaten her daughter. *Don't you ever let my grandchildren go on spring break.*

DeeDee worried, "Are we trollops for interpreting the mooning incident as funny? Have we lost our dignity?"

"Yes," responded Roxie.

DeeDee suggested for the third time since the mooning incident happened that they never speak of it again.

Roxie said, "We have no integrity. You know we will."

They toasted with orange juice, "To no integrity," as the few beer-guzzling spring breakers up by late morning looked on.

* * *

The women picked up Allie for a day of shopping while the groupies played golf. As they pulled into Conner's driveway, a large chicken moseyed across the front lawn, pecking randomly here and there and doing that chicken-neck thing typical of chickens and drug addicts on meth.

As Allie climbed into the car, Roxie asked, "What's up with the Little Red Hen?"

"Conner bought two baby chicks for the grandkids. We planned on eating them eventually, but they graduated to pet status. Gertrude has learned to fly over the cage's fence. I'm afraid if we don't eat her soon, one of the neighbors will. But we just can't bring ourselves to do it. We need to find the hens a home in the country before someone turns us in and the city rounds them up."

Brook claimed post traumatic stress syndrome from the accident the previous day, and refused to drive. She nestled into the back seat, and pulled out her phone.

DeeDee responded, "I've got this." She took the wheel just as Conner rushed out of the house barefooted and chased Gertrude around the yard. Sparky joined in, slipped on the grass, and let loose with a barrage of swear words. The girls watched the rodeo until Gertrude led the men around to the back of the house. Conner hopped awkwardly through gravel rocks on the side of the house while Sparky tried unsuccessfully to use a basketball elbow to take the lead.

Roxie was the first to pull herself together. While loading a Michael Bublé CD, she said. "Let's get out of here before the chicken chasers hurt themselves and we have to deal with that."

Brook recalled having free-range chickens on the farm where she was raised. "You haven't lived until you've had chicken poop squish up between your toes."

"Her kids need to come get her," Roxie said.

DeeDee, desperate to change the subject, said, "If a man lets you borrow his truck, you know you're special."

"Where do you get this shit?"

As DeeDee backed out, Gertrude resurfaced, rounding the corner into the front yard at a full run with the chicken chasers close behind. The girls chanted, "Go, team, go!" out the windows as Michael Bublé crooned on the stereo. Allie noticed a stern-looking neighbor standing on her front porch with hands on her hips. This was worrisome until the lady doubled over with laughter as the chicken headed toward the back yard again with the boys in pursuit.

Brook observed a handsome, gray-haired man across the street stretching his legs for a run. "Holy shit."

"He's a retired Naval officer. He's single," Allie noted.

Restless, Roxie suggested, "Let's put the chicken race in the rearview mirror, girls. We need to be responsible, patriotic consumers and keep this country's economy going."

A few minutes down the road, Brook became contemplative. "I would like to find the kind of man who describes wine as dense and articulate with a hint of oak. . .or something like that. I don't care if he's marginally handsome and not particularly affluent as long as he's interesting."

"Just make sure he's not into chickens," Roxie said.

"Hey, that's my man," Allie responded.

"You're being insensitive, Roxie." DeeDee said.

"Sorry, Allie. I'm not a nice person. I did cry once, though."

"You did not," DeeDee countered.

"Did, too."

"When?"

"When I realized my boobs had taken on the appearance of tube socks filled with sand."

"Oh, my god. You're a hot mess."

Coming out of a meditative state, Brook considered her butterfly status, "You know, I really am happy. I feel like an outside dog who was let inside during an ice storm."

"How did you go from being a butterfly to being an outdoor dog?" Roxie asked.

DeeDee laughed. "Perhaps you have finally found your compass. I still think you should write about your experience."

"The popular writing trend in books is about sci-fi, zombies, vampires, aliens, adventures, or end-of-the-world disasters. I could embrace such a genre, I guess, since my choice of men suggests a symbiotic relationship with demonic mythical beasts. I'm going to title my book, *How I Found Monster Love with a Surly Paranormal*."

"It's nice to see you healing."

A patrolman passed the car, lights flashing. Brook sat up taller in her seat. "Check it out. I love a man in uniform."

Roxie glared. "You are not redeemable."

Brook phoned her daughter back in Oklahoma, who was accustomed to telling her mother such things as, "Don't make me come over there." Her response one day to Brook's announcement that she and her friends had gotten into a food fight in a sushi bar was, "And how old are you people?" Hesitantly, her daughter asked how the trip was going.

Brook reported, "Some redneck in an alligator hat nailed me. No one fell off the balcony onto us. Sparky's off his drugs, and he mooned us. There's a loose chicken in the yard. Gertrude. Don't you ever allow my grandchildren to go on spring break. I have to go. I have another call coming in."

It was Sparky. "I tried calling DeeDee. She won't pick up."

"She's driving."

"Well, you tell her I do not—do you hear—*do not* have pimples on my butt."

Rusty Love

He handed me my heart in jagged shards
Impossible to piece back together   to heal
Broken   I could never love again
Or so I thought

I gave to him   then I was nothing
I stood by him   and he left
Ruined   I could never love again
Or so I thought

With jaded spirit, I moved on   I loved again
Love healed me   then broke me—again
Damaged   No one could love me now
Or so I thought.

The medicine was mine   hurt faded
Forgiveness slithered in, cradling the wounded heart
Lessons   I opened my eyes and my heart
And saw crazy, wonderful rusty love

And so, I can love again.

Chapter 3

Dancing Ho

*There's a dance
in the old gal yet. . . .* Mehitabel

She was once a dancing ho. Her criteria for men whose company she kept was not that they be handsome, compatible, or accomplished in the theater of life. Instead, she required they be masters of the dance—better than she, better than most. Her partner must feel music so intensely that it shoots rhythmically through his body like a current, transferring energy to her with just a touch, an ever-so-subtle lead. He had to be capable of carrying her along with him on a breathless movement marathon—eyes meeting, bodies colliding, pausing, holding, moving in unison.

Such a man was necessary—mandated—because a partner was essential to the dance, which had become a drug so addictive she would pay any price to feed the craving. And so, she became a dancing ho.

Guided by her partner's suggestive pressure on her back or the tension in his hands, they executed steps in partnership—turns, stops, and starts—all emanating not from the feet, but from the core. Every movement of the limbs, the head, and the whole resonated from the power of that core. When their eyes met, the connection was intense, golden, captivating. They were each aware of what the other felt, something unattainable anywhere except in the magnificent throes of the dance. Those watching them—and sometimes moved to applaud—could never imagine or understand the bliss surging through their beings.

She is old now. She does not dance with her body. She dances with her mind. She dances through the medium of memories. Vivid, lush memories—

* * *

A high feasts on her psyche as she enters the dance hall with her partner and lover, both full of anticipation at the prospect of satiating a severe hunger. With his hand in hers, he pulls her urgently and directly onto the dance floor, for that is why they are there—not to drink, not to party—but to dance. Music pounds, whisky-colored lights that dart around like comet tails shine mystically through a haze of smoke, and shadowy figures linger throughout. This is the backdrop for her fix, the setting where the magic happens. She becomes at one with the place.

He leads. She follows. Precisely. Fluently. He initiates a turn, prompts a spin, a snap, a freeze, a head turn, a shoulder shake, a lift of the hip, a flick of the foot—all executed expertly to pulsating music that drives the beauty of the movements and feeds the madness of the dependency the partnership requires. Displaying the style of one confident in his art, he skillfully applies the nuances of syncopated timing, the mark of an expert. Withholding a step like a delayed orgasm, he waits for it, then executes the push and pull of double resistance with an almost frantic movement—crisp, sure.

The genre of the dance and the beat of the music dictate movements, which range from rigid and abrupt to fluid waves. Arms expand and contract with the grace of swirling smoke. Hands curl, flick, grasp, swipe, and snap. Bodies meet in intense but tentative connections that break with a flourish. Heads turn elegantly or with jarring reversals. As fabric sways and flitters like feathers in a soft wind, the dance fills the soul of the dancing ho and satiates an all-consuming addiction.

Bliss, yes, it is bliss. But bliss is experienced only in the moment. It is not sustainable. Bliss must be recreated again and again. So she is tied to her partner. And she does things she shouldn't.

* * *

What was it about the dance that turned her and him into mutual users? What drove her to give herself over to someone she otherwise would not? What made her hang with him in smoky dance halls, ride in his rundown car, tolerate his temperament and, yes, even hop in his bed? It was the bliss. The need. The yearning. The craving for the dance.

When selecting a mate, hunger for that bliss trumped any un-redeeming qualities her partner possessed. He, in turn, tolerated her condescending nature for the sake of the dance. Her superior attitude surfaced everywhere but on the dance floor. There, he became the master. There, he possessed her. There, like a pimp who owned his ho, he owned her. He was her supplier. And they both knew it unequivocally.

She acquiesced to his interpretation of the music, and on the dance floor their bond solidified, night after night. It was also there that bliss exploded, and she felt joy unattainable in any other part of her complicated life. There, her body and mind melded into a glorious, euphoric state of being in the moment.

* * *

Now she is old. Her body, wracked with aches and restricted by limitations, is full of objections. The music and the dance that once meshed together and flowed through her and her partner like shivers are only memories. The rush—so ethereal, yet vivid and potent—will never be experienced again in any setting, except perhaps death.

She contemplates her past and all that life delivered, and she knows if she could pick a moment of her life to live over again, she would choose one in the throes of the dance. She shouldn't. She should select something more universally relevant—a family event, an accomplishment, or a spiritual awakening. But she would choose that moment because she was once a dancing ho. In time relived, she and her partner would own the floor. It would be theirs to take, and they would take it. Together they would capture the night like drug users chasing a high, and she would find bliss—again.

* * *

She is close to nodding off in the lunchroom after a hearty lunch when the assisted-living event planner clinks a glass. "Announcement. Gussy up, ladies and gentlemen. We're going to have a prom Saturday night. Put on your nicest finery. The high school dance band will supply music. Women in the community have donated party dresses. Walkers and canes can be partners. For those of you in wheelchairs, students have volunteered to push and swirl you to the music. Let's all dance."

* * *

She wears a dress that billows freely with the slightest movement. A dapper old man dressed in a dark suit approaches. "Would you like to dance?"

"Sure," she answers, expecting disappointment. The odds of the old fellow delivering a positive experience is remote. She recognizes him as a widowed preacher who is often on an oxygen tank.

Turns out he could execute a pretty good waltz, and her ability to follow, given bad knees and hips, exceeds her expectations. The swishy skirt swirls around her legs, brushing her calves. The soft, flowing fabric billows with each spin and reversal, occasionally tangling loosely in her partner's legs.

"You're a wonderful dancer," she says.

"Thank you. My wife and I used to cut a pretty good rug. You are good yourself."

"I like your tie." It boasts iridescent qualities bold for a preacher.

"Thank you. It's my favorite. My wife gave it to me. She always picked my ties."

The band plays several waltzes throughout the night, and they dance to every one. The partnership becomes more refined with each. Although not exuberant, they are smooth and a tad frisky. When the music transitions to a faster beat, the old fellow demonstrates a flair for showmanship as he introduces jitterbug moves. She responds enthusiastically, revealing considerable stylistic technique. Their joy in the dance resonates with the staff and other dancers who stop to watch. They almost make it to the end of the dance.

She walks the preacher back to his oxygen tank for the last time, hoping she has not killed him. She sits with him while the band plays a salsa number. The exuberant social director occasionally makes loud, Mexican-style screeching noises with her tongue while dancing up a storm. The preacher leans over and whispers in her ear, "I bet she's good in bed." Stunned, she responds, "Pastor, shame on you." And they laugh. They laugh and laugh.

* * *

He dies a few months later. She remembers the sparkle in his eyes when their bodies rose and sank in unison, when they swirled and twirled, when his lead commanded her response, when the magic of the dance defined them. She speculates he was not entirely in the moment, but instead, he reminisced about dancing with his wife. She knows this because she was recalling her days as a dancing ho. The source of the gleeful emotions expressed through their twinkling eyes as they danced did not matter. Bliss was re-lived, a craving satisfied—somewhat.

She is hoping for another prom. She may be in a wheelchair by then with a young whipper-snapper pushing her in circles. In the meantime, she will dance in her memories— the music like love songs tapping on her shoulder. In whatever fashion the dance is accomplished, it will be magical and blissful because she is, after all, a dancing ho—still.

The Dance

The swish
The swirl
The twirl
The turn
The spin
The extension
The flick
The shift
The push
The pull
The connecting
The letting go
The magic
The spell
The high
The bliss
The dance
Oh, yes, the dance

Chapter 4

Beyond Dirty Dancing

The high concept of hunching.

My girlfriend and I were dancing down cowboys at a Dallas dance hall when the music switched from country to some sort of bump and grind noise. I call it hunching music. Young people, who had been waiting for this moment, swooped in and filled the dance floor. Thrashing, humping, and bumping began with a vengeance, a behavior that reveals a defect in the fabric of society. Before you conclude I'm a hysterical prude, let me describe the action.

Lines formed of guys and gals gyrating to the beat of the music, grinding butts into the persons behind them and/or thrusting crotches into the butts of the persons in front of them, whichever way you choose to interpret the movement. Boy on girl, girl on boy, girl on girl, boy on boy—their version of a conga line perhaps. Couples hooked up. Girls squatted down to put their heads in their partners' crotches in what was without doubt some kind of near-sex experience. Guys were thrusting at any part of a girl's anatomy they could get at. Girl-on-girl action had men on the sidelines spellbound.

I had seen this kind of dancing before, but not to this degree. Such antics were even evident at my daughter's California wedding party when the bridesmaids hunched the groom on the dance floor. A few drinks later, my daughter spanked the maid of honor to the beat of the music. I chastised her, "You lesbians stop that. Your grandmother is here." Her cousins, who lived in rural Iowa, had mixed responses. The women seemed befuddled while the guys, wide-eyed and riveted, no doubt, envied the groom.

Recognizing each generation embraces its own rebellious craze, one that challenges the bounds of respectability, I try to be openminded about the enthusiasm for oversexed dancing. But there is a false equivalency when the bopping about movements of rock and roll or the sensuous ones of disco are compared to humping madness. If I were to describe the hunching to someone of my generation who has not seen it, I could take them down a dark hole.

I prefer to remain on the fringe of such outrageous currents of change. When entering nightclub environments, a woman of my generation must take a defensive stance and display a "don't fuck with me, buddy" persona. I introduce this strategy early on, lest I end up with a perfectly executed spin being interrupted by some guy grabbing my waist and humping my backside, in which case I would have to kill him. When a man asks me to dance, I point to the young dancers humping away and warn the fellow up front, "We won't be doing that."

The excesses of the Texas club that night took on a particularly rank quality. The "children" were endlessly resourceful at inventing sexually charged dance moves. Although grossed out by the display, I stared like an outdoor dog whose owners were eating steak on the other side of the patio window. The whacked out, orgy-esque nature of what was happening on the dance floor struck me as repulsive and compelling at the same time. A frantic and out of control situation, it is impossible to describe it adequately. What we have here is a failure of children to remember they have parents.

A couple right in front of us entered into such a flamboyant erotic state that she bent forward and placed her hands on the floor while grinding her butt into her partner's crotch. She flipped her hair wildly as he pounded her. He periodically grabbed her hair, pulled her head back, and rode her like a pony. The pair had clearly lost their moral bearings. As I gave thanks for clothes, I concluded it was true what some people say, "Texas is Baja Oklahoma," meaning Oklahoma has its issues but things are worse down there. (My apologies to my Texas friends.)

My girlfriend and I sat frozen on our bar stools. About that time, some man tapped me on the shoulder. "Would you like to dance?"

Instead of saying, "You are kidding, right?" I said, "Aw, hell, no!" I didn't mean to be impolite. The response was spontaneous. It didn't even come close, though, to expressing the apprehension swirling in my head, which was something similar to the heebie-jeebies one feels when a tickle on the neck turns out to be a spider.

I must have been overzealous in my reaction because the guy said, "I didn't ask you to fuck. I just asked you to dance."

I didn't believe him. In lieu of tasing him, I asked "Doesn't anyone ever do the Shottish anymore?" He threw up his hands and walked away, which was a good thing. I was prepared to go all Oklahoma bat-shit crazy on the guy.

As a person in the third trimester of life, making social observations is like waiting for a restroom door to open and some guy comes out like Ace Ventura, holding his breath and waving his hand in front of his face while saying, "I can't believe I did that. Don't go in there."

The children consider my dancing passé, and my daughter once begged, "Please, Mom, don't spin." But my plan is to maintain the conventions of my age group no matter how disenfranchised I get. I'm not one to adopt the decorum of a politician's wife, but I'm also not going beyond the bounds of a Tina Turner dance move either. The young folks might have lowered the bar, but I'm not ducking under it.

Chapter 5

Grumpy or Grateful—a Choice

It is not happiness that makes you grateful.
It is gratefulness that makes you happy. . .
Brother David Steindle-Rast

Do not assume it is human ecology to be grumpy when you are old. Except in cases of mental or physiological deterioration, grumpiness is a choice. Gratefulness is the antidote.

Being grumpy is aging disrespectfully. Everyone has their sour moments, though. People are flawed, and dispositions constantly tested. In spite of these challenges, a robust, rewarding, and purposeful aging experience is possible.

A person cannot be perpetually grumpy and remain connected to others. People will shut the person out. An old lady, who groused about everything, complained her son never came to visit her. He explained why: "Mom can suck the life out of me in five minutes." She had specific gripes like,

"Those damn fruit flies are all over my peaches," and "Those men only bring rolls to the pot luck dinners." Then there were the more quintessential complaints like, "No matter where I go, there are people there."

Connecting with others in a positive way sparks happiness while romancing the negative promotes a sour disposition and loneliness. Unhappiness is inevitable in this scenario. Why would anyone choose that? Doing so is a self-centered decision. It feeds the egocentric need to feel justified in interpreting situations as abusive while ignoring the impact such interpretations have on everyone else. Being grumpy implies a lack of empathy for others.

* * *

Why are people grumpy? Two basic emotions drive behavior: fear and love. Grumpiness reflects fear and induces isolation while gratitude promotes love and a cheerful, hopeful nature that encourages connections. Which emotion is chosen defines the present and predetermines the future. The complaints of grumpy people are tragically predictive of future unfortunate negative outcomes.

Madelyn visited Wilber, a prickly old fellow who bombarded her with a substantial dose of complaints. His cantankerous nature was so severe that she suspected he possessed a gray aura. Nestled in a well-worn, overstuffed chair, he said, "I don't like nobody." The crotchety old codger delivered his next reflection in a long menu of complaints,

"And I don't like dogs." The man interjected a testy comment about the weather before moving on to this: "I don't like morning people—or mornings—or people."

When Madelyn departed, she said, "Have a nice day."

Wilber responded, "I have other plans."

His complaints were tragically intriguing and often entertaining, but any fascination had limits. When a person is in a grouchy state, vicious cycles of fatalism hover like angry demons, isolation sets in, and the person becomes old too soon.

Contrast this with a grateful person who shines and sparkles, one who enhances the lives of others just by their way of being in the world. The gap between projecting grumpiness rather than gratefulness is significant. How would Madelyn have felt if Wilber had been pleasant and grateful?

Some people are wired for grumpiness. It has been said mean old people were once mean young people. This raises the question: Is it possible to choose one's disposition? Although it is not possible to eliminate innate tendencies, and it is a challenge to change old patterns, most people are capable of choosing their behavior. Doing so requires intention: hate or benevolence, grumpiness or gratefulness.

Grumpy people are decidedly egocentric, as is demonstrated by an elderly woman who engaged a young man to assist her with errands. He watched her try to persuade a receptionist in her doctor's office to let her in ahead of others in the waiting room. Later she took off with amazing speed, given her crippled state, to beat someone to a grocery store door. While in traffic, she complained, "Those people are in our way." Lunch was tarnished by a series of complaints ranging from the waitress' lipstick color to the brand of jelly. Her sense of entitlement and lack of awareness of others stunned the young man. An astute fellow, he noted that significant insecurities plagued her, as did fear.

Our culture is an obstacle to gratefulness because it encourages a victim mentality. Victims are continuously identifying persecutors who are abusing them. Bleeding and clotting, they never heal. These sufferers must prove their toughness by constantly fighting for respect. Choked by insecurities and the fear that they don't deserve it, they become preoccupied with perceived offenses. Constantly on guard, their combative demands for respect make them so testy they drive people away.

In spite of their behavior, grumpy people are deserving of love. Giving it will often turn them around, at least temporarily. And why not do that? Love is the reason Madelyn will visit Wilber again in spite of his cranky moods. And, because his unpleasantness has driven so many others away, those visits take on even more significance.

* * *

The consequence of choosing grumpiness or gratefulness flows through generations. People may have little influence on when and how things happen, but on some level, most have control over how they deal with losses, health issues, and dying. Younger people observe the choices of older folks, how they live and die, and interpret their own futures through those observations. These impressions are especially significant because they create legacy. Legacies pass from generation to generation, so they are forever.

A person's temperament is reflected in their appearance. When conducting workshops on aging, an instructor could look out over a field of participants the first day and instantly determine the temperament of the grumpy and the grateful. Peppered about were always a few ill-tempered souls who scowled at her and others, their faces and body language in a constant state of rigid defensiveness. Then there were the grateful folks whose sparkling eyes and eager expressions fueled the instructor's enthusiasm. As participants' stories were revealed over the course of the workshop, the interpretations the instructor made on the first day, based solely on appearances, were confirmed.

Grouchy people don't realize, or care, that it is important to people who care about them that they be okay. They are not okay, so they create burdens for the ones they are supposed to care about most. How sad is that?

* * *

The challenges to maintaining a grateful frame of reference as one ages are brutal. Denial is not a good method for avoiding a negative temperament. It is lying to oneself and to others. Acceptance is the key to avoiding denial. Consider this: A seventy-year-old man in denial lies about his age and brags, "I'm *sixty*, and I run five miles a day." A more impressive statement comes from the truth, "I'm *seventy*, and I run five miles a day."

When older people get together, discussions of health issues often take off like lap cars spotting a green flag. Oversharing of details about aches and pains is why young people never ask an older person how they feel. No one wants a play-by-play of a colonoscopy. One lady interrupts such conversations with, "Speaking of sex. . ." Most people her age don't have much to say about sex, but the suggestion generates laughs, and the subject changes.

How one interprets situations is key. An old lady who embraced gratefulness said, "When a driver pulls out in front of me, rather than thinking, 'What an idiot,' I think, 'I did that once.' I'm thankful it wasn't me who did it this time, and I'm just grateful I can still drive."

To avoid being sucked into the grumpy zone, it's helpful to develop coping mechanisms. Two words help: *oh well.* Effective medicine is dispensed through a well-timed *oh well* when back fat materializes, short-term memory fails, body parts move around (downward mostly), or a body becomes so broken it is as though it came from IKEA and someone put it together without instructions. The *oh well* neutralizes disturbing observations and promotes acceptance. It's okay at some point, for an old person to conclude they are *not sorry* for unfortunate circumstances they cannot control, such as memory losses that cause them to disappoint. Apologies can be replaced with such comments as, "When you are my age, you'll understand."

Another approach is to interpret inevitable degradation of the body as patina. Copper takes on a green tone called patina as it weathers. Many consider it beautiful. Imperfections on furniture, accessories, buildings, and just about anything can be interpreted as patina. Blemishes are evidence of history—proof the object has endured and is valued, used, and beautifully flawed. A new version of beauty is embraced when the concept of patina is applied to the body.

It would be misguided, though, to suggest that all visible signs of aging are beautiful. They are not. But they are organic and pure and part of still being here. When challenges threaten to take a person's disposition down a dark path, a rally is possible by remembering that aging is a gift, one not everyone gets.

Avoiding grumpiness often requires bold choices. It is common for people to self-limit and fail to realize the broad spectrum of alternatives available to them. Exploring options outside of one's comfort zone often reveals imaginative solutions.

An old W. C. Fields movie illustrates an interesting and outrageous response to a situation. Out on a Sunday drive, Fields and his girlfriend were repeatedly bullied by road hogs. Frustrated, they purposely ran into one. The girlfriend was wealthy, so they went to a dealership, bought another car, and went searching for more road hogs to run into. Several cars were demolished and new ones bought that day. They had a high old time. Perhaps this is a poor example. No one would recommend this strategy, but it illustrates the broad range of choices available when options are explored creatively. Fresh ways of responding to life experiences can yield surprising positive outcomes.

* * *

Gratefulness is the key to a happy spirit. It is free and available to everyone. Although there is always something to be upset about, few circumstances are worthy of an ill-tempered response. Instead of being irritated in noisy restaurants and public places, the hustle and bustle can be interpreted as energy—a buzzing around in which a person doesn't have to participate but in the center of which they can thrive. Instead of rushing around, retired people can let people in work clothes running errands on their lunch hour or mothers with small children ahead of them in lines in stores.

A young man bumped into an older woman in a store and said, "Sorry, granny." Initially, the lady bristled, but after observing the kid bungling his way through the store, it became obvious he was a hapless, charming mess. Perceiving him as some mother's beloved son and a grandmother's adored grandson, the lady judged him less harshly, and "granny" became a compliment.

Humor can be an effective antidote to young people pushing an older person's cranky button. A man, irritated that his grandson wore his pants so low his underwear showed, was tempted to lecture the kid. Instead he pursued a more creative approach. He persuaded relatives to wear low-slung pants with underwear revealed to a family dinner—an intervention of sorts. Children, women, and old folks waddled around with pant crotches almost to their knees. Baby diapers were even riding low. Colorful, playful underwear and even a few butt cracks were revealed.

This was a hoot. Pictures were taken, memories made, and an episode of lectures and disapproval, which would have surely provoked a rebellion, were replaced with fun and laughter. No doubt, the grandson's connection with his grandfather blossomed as a result of this unique and entertaining way of sending a message. Laughter is like frosting on the cake of living in the moment.

Health issues are ripe for the introduction of humor. Some older people are offended by "old people" jokes and young folks often don't get the joke. Comedic efforts at the expense of older people can be trite and some are downright insulting. But you gotta give it to the guy who said to the doctor doing his colonoscopy, "Could you write a note for my wife saying my head is not up there?" And who wouldn't laugh when an elderly lady gets into a car thinking her son is picking her up only to discover she has hopped into the vehicle of the Archbishop who asked, "Are you going home with me?"

Solutions to aging issues—and any other problem, actually—reside in the context of connectedness. An ancient philosopher said, "There are no others." This concept acknowledges the connectedness of everyone and every living thing in the universe. It implies that every action, interaction, expression, and example of resilience has implications for the whole. Each person is a part of something bigger than themselves, and every person's actions are meaningful and relevant to the whole. When adopting a "there are no others" philosophy, a person is kind, generous, protective, and respectful of others. He becomes an expert at coping because his position in the universe makes sense, and he knows he matters in the grand scheme of things. He shines as a beacon of hope. Service to others proliferates. Gratefulness abounds. And grumpiness is not on the agenda.

Aging carves deep veins of wisdom into a person's psyche. The challenge lies in tapping into that and sharing it—in other words, making a difference. The following story is about two women who chose positive reactions to an incident ripe with prospects for negative ones. Their ways of being in the world reflect grateful dispositions as opposed to grumpy ones, and their responses demonstrate a playful sense of connectedness.

———————

Tango was a farm dog, a free-range mutt accustomed to rambling uninhibited. He existed in a world rich with adventure and void of discipline. My brother brought Tango along when he visited me in the city. A leash was outside the realm of possibilities for Tango, and as soon as he exited my brother's truck, he took off after a rabbit in the neighbor's yard.

After several zig-zag runs, he and the rabbit rampaged frantically in circles around a fountain. My neighbor, Mollie, had just planted rows of flowers there. Dirt and flowers flew as though an explosion had gone off, creating a debris field several yards wide in all directions. Horrified, I surveyed the mess. Since Mollie and I had a friendly gardening competition going on, my response was inappropriate. I laughed.

I chastised myself for not having more compassion as I worked up the courage to confess to Mollie what had happened to desecrate her flowerbed. And I hoped I could do so without laughing.

Fortunately, Mollie was a person who lived in a state of gratefulness. She answered her door laughing heartily and said, "I was making coffee and saw the chaos out of the kitchen window. It was hilarious—like something out of a cartoon."

Ah, a burden lifted. As I sat drinking coffee with Mollie before we replanted flowers, I considered how grateful I was to have her as a neighbor and a friend. Then she said, "You know, my geraniums out back are doing much better than yours this year." *Oh no you didn't.* And the banter began. I liked Mollie. She was a nice lady and a good neighbor, but it was not true what she said about those geraniums.

I've Been Mom-ed

Years were invested in trying not to be like her.
I criticized her choices and devalued her contributions.
Rejecting her lifestyle and the image she projected,
I thrashed against the chains she accepted.

Her harsh innuendos and criticisms cut deep.
Judgment of me provoked a rebel spirit.
So I stayed away, relishing the privilege of independence.
I didn't need her, or so I thought.

Then I hit bottom, crashed and burned I did.
A fortress between me and the abyss, she saved me.
I rallied, steadfast and fierce.
And when I did, I became the best of her.

(Many of the incidents described here are based on the antics of my dad, whose quirky nature and notorious sense of humor amused all who knew him. However, because Dad possessed a level of dignity Skillet did not embrace, I took fictional liberties with Skillet's personality, accent, and actions. The family dynamics in this concocted story are similar to those I experienced as a member of a large family growing up on an Iowa farm in the 1950s. However—just for fun—I turned myself into a boy here. I used my Aunt Weezie's name because it seemed to fit with Skillet. This character is not her, although she gave me one of the best lines in this piece.)

Chapter 6

Uncle Skillet

Sometimes love is unpretentious.

Uncle Skillet spray-painted the plumes on pampas grass growing along the road an iridescent pink. When Dad turned into Skillet's driveway, I spotted him lounging in a rocking chair on the front porch of his trailer house. Dressed in coveralls, a shirt with cut-off sleeves, and a well-worn cap, he looked like Larry the Cable Guy. Skillet delighted in watching cars slow down to gawk at the vibrant blooms. Occasionally, a car stopped, backed up, and entered the driveway, its passengers on a quest for seeds. Skillet directed them to the paint section of the local hardware store.

Five of us kids, ranging in age from three to thirteen, were packed into Dad's old Ford clunker. It was the pre-seatbelt era, and we hung out of windows and fought over nirvana—the shelf space along the backseat window. As a ten-year-old boy, third in rank, I was generally lost in the shuffle of siblings. Dennis, Daisy, and I were routinely bullied by older brother Dwayne. I called him Doowayne as a measure of disrespect because he had a habit of twisting my arm behind my back until I said whatever word he demanded—words like fart and wingding. Three-year-old Drew was a general nuisance to us older boys. We ran him off by telling him, "Mom is calling you."

We were sticky from a trip to the Dairy Queen. The criterion for winning ice cream races took a dramatic turn one day when Daisy, the last to finish, bragged she still had ice cream when the rest of us did not. This introduced a paradigm shift. When we arrived at Skillet's place, cones were soft and ice cream dripped from hands as we each avoided the last bite. This sent Mom into a tither. "Aunt Weezie will have a conniption fit."

* * *

We kids were fascinated by Uncle Skillet, who had a knack for entertaining children. Bending rules was his game. To reduce the cost of admission when he took us to drive-in movies, Dennis and I hid under a blanket on the floorboard of the backseat of his old Plymouth. Doowayne, Daisy, and little Drew sat innocently in the seat. Aunt Weezie, a woman of principle, fidgeted nervously in the passenger seat. Doowayne, quick to take advantage and knowing we could not respond, landed several kicks, so we waffled around under the blanket until Skillet gave us the all clear.

Skillet's antics placed Aunt Weezie in a frequent state of intervention, like when he displayed Christmas decorations of reindeer fornicating in the front yard. Her occasional verbal lashings had little effect on Skillet's behavior. There wasn't much he took seriously, and messing with Weezie was his favorite pastime. He claimed to have married her because she had freckles on her butt and she was purdy. I knew from Weezie's response to that remark—a fierce glare—Skillet had crossed a line, although I was not sure what that line was.

To Weezie's chagrin, Skillet used swear words in ranting, rhythmic strings of dialogue. He defended this verbal dexterity by labeling such words *sentence enhancers*. He rationalized, "Wawl, if yous sits on a cat or cuts off a leg with a chainsaw, swearing is da only way ter deal wif dat." He moderated his swearing around children by using nonsensical words like "Oh shirt," "Dame it," "Son of a Witch," or a whole string of babble. I recognized them as bad words, though, from the tone and the circumstances under which they were uttered.

In spite of surface tension in their relationship, Skillet fancied his woman. All he ever wanted was her respect, and he was on the cusp of obtaining it most of his life. He stole her years ago from a well-off boyfriend who collected Elvis paraphernalia and played the blues on a ukulele. Weezie had a taste for the novel. Skillet's playful quirkiness and disarming humor won out over the other fellow's wealth. Any disapproval she exhibited about Skillet's antics belied a deep affection. She often said, "Skillet's bad qualities are a gift."

Although Mom disapproved of Skillet's not-so-fine qualities, she harbored considerable affection for him. Her concern was his ability to influence her husband. She complained to Dad, "Skillet could pee on your leg and convince you it's raining." She called Skillet "batshit crazy" when he fried up calf testicles and fed them to her misrepresented as something similar to Chicken McNuggets. On another occasion, she called him a bullshit aficionado, to which he responded, "Thank ya, ma'am."

Uncle Skillet was different from Dad, even though they were brothers. Skillet was an eccentric, zany fellow who saw the novelty in everything while Dad was staid and predictable. They complemented each other, though. Skillet's enthusiastic quirkiness and marginal good judgment were balanced by Dad's common sense. As the voice of reason, Dad reined Skillet in when antics threatened to backfire and rescued him when he stepped in trouble.

We kids used to say, "Uncle Skillet is c-a-a-r-a-z-y," and many who knew him would support that position. Some concluded he was one watt short of a nightlight, but he wasn't dumb in the IQ sense of the word. He was just different. I suspect his greatest fear was being ordinary.

Weezie conformed to local customs. Skillet did not. It wasn't in his character to aspire to conquer the hurdle of respectability, so he did things he shouldn't. He stole things—minor things. He did so as a prank as opposed to any motivation to acquire. In his mind, sneaking away with something was an adrenaline-fueled hoax. He blamed his behavior on "dain bramage" from a plumbing incident. Most people in his small community knew him and didn't take his antics seriously. Instead, they considered him "a character" and relished sharing tales of his exploits.

Skillet was candid about his obsessions. If asked what kind of Christmas tree he had, he answered, "stolen"—an honest response. He stole balloons from car lots for Weezie's birthdays and picked flowers from neighbors' yards for anniversaries. A neighbor lady told Weezie about discovering Skillet tromping around in her flowerbed. When she yelled at him, he responded, "I ain't stealin' no chickens" and continued picking peonies. Weezie chastised him about this transgression. He responded, "I's gots through life wiffn out bein' arrested. So there's that."

Aunt Weezie's meticulous nature contrasted sharply with Skillet's messy, helter-skelter disposition. An avid tinkerer, his compulsion to collect things and reinvent them caused the world outside their trailer to emerge as the antithesis of the orderly interior. He called the city dump *The Mall*. Junk accumulated in sheds, and metal objects dotted the landscape causing the property to resemble the debris field of an airplane crash.

Weezie protected her territory. "Skillet, you cannot store car parts in the bathtub." Skillet occasionally tested her resolve by introducing one of his treasures into the trailer. He paid a severe price for such transgressions. Weezie retaliated by putting makeup in his tool box. Skillet didn't react to this tactic. So she resorted to conniption fits.

He brought a basketball scoreboard buzzer home from *The Mall* and sat it on the kitchen table. A plain metal box with a plug-in cord protruding from the back, it sparked Skillet's curiosity. He was determined to figure out what it was. We kids were visiting. Fascinated, we hovered around the table to examine it, nudging each other for position. Weezie stood by in an apron over a floral dress resembling wallpaper, hands on her hips. A dishtowel dangled from one hand. When Skillet plugged the device in, a horrific noise blared forth. Everyone jumped. Kitchen chairs flew over, sister Daisy cried, Dennis fell on his butt, Drew wet his pants, and Weezie launched into a conniption fit extraordinaire, which involved frantically waiving the dishtowel. Skillet calmly gave his interpretation of the device. "That's some noisy doohickey."

Uncle Skillet was known for such zingers—short, pithy musings that summed up situations perfectly. Following any kind of epic failure, of which there were many in his world, he described the situation with, "Well, that was weird."

He hit a deer and loaded it into the car to take home and butcher. Turns out the deer was not dead. Skillet scrambled to exit the vehicle as flailing hooves broke windows and tore up upholstery. Finally, the deer escaped. Skillet summed up the deer's position. "He wanted out."

Skillet was a mechanic. When he went to a car junkyard for parts, he usually bought the entire car. Junk vehicles peppered the landscape around the trailer, much to Aunt Weezie's dismay. When she insisted he stop the madness, Skillet hid acquisitions behind a grove of trees. When the leaves fell off in the fall, Weezie had a conniption fit. His car collection provided the equivalent of an auto parts store. When a car he or Weezie drove failed, he moved on to whichever junker in his collection was the easiest to fix. That vehicle became their mode of transportation until the next mechanical failure. None of the tires on his cars matched, upholstery was optional, and the paint color of doors, hoods, and trunk lids often contrasted with the rest of the body.

Skillet named his cars. An old Ford called Delbert was rigged so Skillet could steer it with a tool attached to the steering column. This allowed him to remove the steering wheel, hand it to a passenger, and deliver a zinger, "I'm tired of driving." When the Ford overheated once too often, an old Plymouth rigged to dispense Jack Daniels through a dashboard spout took its place. He named it Flo.

One old car was gutted except for the front seat. We kids loved crawling into the trunk space, which Skillet named *The Vaginia* (as in almost vagina). This caused both Mom and Weezie to have an impassioned fit. Skillet came as close to an apology as I'd ever heard over that. He explained his faux pas, "I's has *dain bramage."* The trunk was re-named *Anus*, which drew a similar response. Weezie called him a special kind of stupid. His defense: "I ain't never been arrested." Finally, he named it Pluto-Uto-Noono, a moniker that met the women's approval and resinated so well with us kids that we gave the name to one of our farm cats. As we followed him out the door after Weezie's scolding, we were on our way to help Skillet turn the toolshed into the Cook County Jail. Skillet said, "Well, kids, I just took one for the team." I wasn't sure what he meant by that, but I was certain he was my hero.

Skillet was a bully on the road. Everyone had a nicer car than he did, so he always had the right of way. He was merciless at intersections. Drivers braked and glared. After close calls, Skillet said to unnerved passengers, "I've got a whole passel of cars." He celebrated close calls by singing "King of the Road."

Skillet loved to con kids. He convinced Drew that a skunk roaming the property was a cat named *Eeeew*. He climbed into our treehouse and pulled the ladder up, leaving us pacing below. He demanded a password. *Vaginia* and *Anus* were unsuccessful. *Fart* worked, and we were admitted, except for Drew whose mom was calling him.

A neighbor boy had a habit of ringing the doorbell and asking Weezie if Skillet could come out and play. The kid had a limp because his dad ran over him in the driveway when he was a toddler. With extreme irreverence, Skillet named him Speedbump, which amazingly caught on with the kid's family and probably scarred him for life.

Speedbump didnd't believe it when Skillet told the boy he had a twin brother named Bucket. "The only way folks can tells us apart," Skillet said, "is that I's wears my cap frontwards and Bucket wears his backwards." The kid was not convinced, so Skillet suggested Speedbump check out Bucket, who was working on the other side of the barn. The boy headed off to do so. Skillet dropped his shovel, turned his hat around, grabbed a pitchfork, and ran to the other side of the barn. Soon thereafter, he darted back, dropped the pitchfork, turned his hat frontward and picked up the shovel just as Speedbump rounded the building. I decided Uncle Skillet was some sort of god.

* * *

We were wild. Dad warned us when we arrived at destinations, "Don't act normal," except when at Uncle Skillet's. There we were allowed to run amuck. So as we poured out of Dad's Ford that day, we scattered like a covey of quail, eager to explore Skillet's wonderland.

Obsessed with cleanliness, Weezie herded us one-by-one into the bathroom where she scrubbed away sticky ice cream residue and crusty farm dirt. We exited covered with red blotches and smelling of Jergen's Lotion. Mom tolerated Weezie's fastidiousness. It wasn't that Mom didn't want her children clean. She did, but she was an overwhelmed farm woman with chores and five kids. And she was pregnant again.

While Mom and Aunt Weezie puttered in the kitchen, I hung around long enough to steal a cookie. I heard Mom tell

Weezie she got pregnant helping Dad quit smoking. I didn't know how that worked, but Dad did stop smoking.

Skillet showed Dad his latest invention in the workshop before leading him to the backyard. We kids tagged along, bouncing off each other like pinballs, except for Drew, whose mother was calling him. There we discovered a new deck constructed of wooden pallets stolen from the alleys in town that Skillet canvassed daily before exploring *The Mall*. On the deck sat a charcoal cooker made from a converted barrel (a dump find). A brisket mounted on a rotisserie rod (a dump find) attached to an old Black and Decker drill (a dump find) rotated at a remarkable speed over charcoals. Dad's jaw dropped when he saw the apparatus.

Meat juice flew everywhere, splashing against the trailer and coating a mutt named Rufus (a dump find), who made a valiant effort to catch liquid morsels midair. Barnyard cats hovered on the fringes of the action, looking confused but anticipatory.

"That meat is going to be dry," Skillet said.

"You think?" Dad responded.

When flames began shooting out of the barrel from grease splattered onto charcoals, Uncle Skillet attempted to close the lid to smother the flames. This caused the drill to break loose from its moorings and vibrate against the metal barrel, creating a thunderous noise. Weezie and Mom rushed from the kitchen just as the drill escaped the barrel, tumbled to the ground, and flopped around like a chicken with its head cut off. We children froze in a state of shock and awe as our supper was thrashed around in dirt and grass. Cats slunk backward as Rufus went nuts, barking as though he'd treed a coon. The women's admonitions complicated the scenario but had little influence on Skillet, who relished the slapstick nature of the situation.

Rufus managed to sporadically latch onto the brisket, but the drill put up a good fight. For a minute, it appeared as though the drill and brisket team would win. Skillet danced a jig while dodging the ramped-up canine and pursuing the flailing drill. After several attempts, he landed the contraption and turned it off. He removed the dirt- and grass-encrusted meat from the rotisserie rod and tossed it to Rufus, who eyed encroaching cats menacingly as he gnawed away. Skillet announced, "It woulda been a lots better fight if'n there was mud." Weezie entered the trailer, slamming the screen door—hard.

As Uncle Skillet drove to town to buy roasted chicken for supper, we kids and Rufus tagged along. Riding in Uncle Skillet's car was often an adventure. Anytime we piled into one of his vehicles, he announced, "We're off to St. Louis." I harbored grand illusions of someday actually going to St. Louis, wherever that was.

As Skillet sang his favorite song, "Dead Skunk in the Middle of the Road, Stinkin' to High Heaven," we passed a neighbor's house. Their dog, Dixie, dashed out to chase the car. Uncle Skillet slammed on the brakes, bringing it to a sudden stop. Dixie, having had this experience before, followed her customary protocol. She circled the car, jumping up again and again as though on a trampoline, peering into windows. This provoked hilarious laughter from us kids and drove Rufus into a frenzy.

Eventually, Dixie gave up and slunk away, looking back occasionally, a scowl on her face—at least as close to one as a dog can get. She plunked down on her belly, panting profusely. Skillet said, "Watch this." He peeled out, and Dixie resumed the chase. Little faces peered out the back window as Dixie galloped desperately through the dust, her long black coat rippling in the wind as she faded into the distance.

On the ride home, my siblings and I occupied ourselves with keeping Rufus out of the roasted chicken. During supper, Uncle Skillet boasted that the chicken didn't suck. He asked Dad to help pull up marijuana weeds growing wild along the south fence line. "I can help," said Doowayne, demonstrating rare enthusiasm for physical labor.

In an effort to manage Doowayne's expectations, Skillet explained that although this weed bore the exotic name, it grew wild and produced no worthy buds. Doowayne was missing the gene that supported rational thinking. With the excitement of a biology freak who found a tarantula in the bathtub, he imagined the prospect of acquiring the Holy Grail of pot inventory.

Soon a motherload of marijuana weeds nestled in a pile in Skillet's yard where it was left to dry enough for burning. A sweaty, hyped-up Doowayne tried to no avail to persuade Mom and Dad to load some into the trunk of their car. Uncle

Skillet alleviated his disappointment by promising Doowayne he could come over in a few days and sniff the smoke as the weed pile burned. Later that evening, as Mom checked Doowayne for ticks, he said, "I sure do like Uncle Skillet. I like Aunt Weezie, too. She has freckles on her butt."

* * *

One night Dad got an urgent call from Weezie. She wouldn't say what was wrong but pleaded, "Come quick." We rushed over to discover Uncle Skillet stuck upside down in the belly of a steel commercial furnace in the front yard. The old, rusty apparatus resembled a huge upside-down funnel, narrowing to a peak at the top for a chimney hookup. Legs protruding from the top were all we could see of Skillet. Swear words echoed from inside. It sounded as though his head was in a bucket. The rant comforted us kids. Skillet wasn't dead.

He had acquired the old furnace from the dump and used it to keep Rufus and cats from getting at orphaned baby pheasants he was raising. Weezie explained, "He came home drunk, removed the screen from the top to feed the pheasants, and fell in headfirst." His stomach stopped his descent. Skillet could have died if she hadn't looked out the window and spotted his flailing legs.

As the fervor of Skillet's rant faded, Dad's adrenalin kicked in. He located a tire jack and elevated one side of the funnel. This provided enough leverage for him and Doowayne to tip the monster over.

They still couldn't extricate Skillet, so Weezie put a foot on each side of the furnace opening and pulled hard. Soon Skillet popped out. Weezie said, "I feel like I just birthed a baby when I didn't even know I was pregnant." Skillet sat on the ground—red faced, legs splayed out in front of him—looking dumbfounded. When he rallied enough to speak, he said, "I gots drunk, and den dis happened."

When the furnace tilted, baby pheasants scurried about like puppies who found a gate open. Rufus's bird dog inclinations kicked in, and we kids went into rescue mode. Doowayne wrestled a fledgling from Rufus's jaws, and I kicked the hound soundly as he launched after another one. Soon a confined Rufus barked and banged against the toolshed door as we kids caged chicks in a cardboard box and carried it into Weezie's kitchen. She was pouring coffee down a plastered Skillet —who should have been contrite, but was not.

Weezie didn't like it when she was mad and Skillet didn't notice. He made a point of not noticing. "It was like I was a weird yard ornament," he said to Dad. Then he looked at a scowling Weezie, winked, and said, "You's prettier than a can a pork n' beans."

She glared at him for a moment before launching into a ranting, raving conniption fit so severe it drove Rufus under the table. Suddenly, her voice quivered. Tears streamed down her face. Skillet lowered his head for a minute and then got up and hugged her. It's the only time I ever saw them hug. Dad said,

"Let's go." We scurried out, leaving a box of peeping chicks on the kitchen counter

* * *

I was fifteen when Uncle Skillet got sick. He made the mistake of saying he wanted to die. Weezie, a large, well-endowed woman, threatened to throw herself on him and smother him. Hearty laughter was out of his grasp, but he managed a grin. He died soon thereafter. We all sang "Dead Skunk in the Middle of the Road" at his funeral.

Dad and we kids spent hours loading stuff from the debris field onto trucks to be hauled off. A man took the junk vehicles away. Dwayne manicured the landscape. He pulled weeds along the fence line, occasionally wiping watery eyes with the sleeves of his shirt. The place spruced up good and sold quickly to some man who admired the pallet patio. Aunt Weezie moved into an apartment in town. We visited her there often.

* * *

Much older now, I'm married with kids. I often promise them a trip to St. Louis when they get into the car. We've had several generations of cats named Pluto-Uto-Noono. Much to my kids' delight, I planted pampas grass on my property this year and spray-painted the plumes iridescent pink. My wife picked a few for the house. I would take some to Weezie, but I worry they would make her sad.

I still call my older brother Doowayne (affectionately). He calls his oldest son Bucket. Dennis is a carpenter, and Drew is in college. Daisy, a veterinarian, is raising baby pheasants because a city-slicker motorcyclist hit and killed their mother believing he had struck a peacock.

Dad created a decked-out street rod from one of Skillet's old cars. He named it Zinger after rejecting my suggestion that he name it Anus. He and Mom show it off at car shows. Drew drove his girlfriend to the prom in it. When we kids ride in it, we sing "King of the Road."

I stop in occasionally at the apartment for a Weezie fix. I bring her cashew brittle from an Amish bakery, and she makes me peach-flavored tea. I help her with odd jobs and a jigsaw puzzle, being careful not to find too many pieces and steal her thunder. She hides a puzzle piece to assure she gets to put in the last one and declare, "I won," just like Skillet used to do.

No longer under the shadow of Skillet's big personality, Weezie has blossomed. In a sense, she has taken over for him. Her chitchat is flush with zingers and robust memories. On my last visit, she asked, "Remember when Skillet bought me a huge teddybear to carry around at the fair? When someone asked where he won it, he said, 'At Sears.'"

"Yeah. Remember when he bought Daisy one?"

"Yes. She strutted around the midway, the envy of all her friends."

I laughed. "Remember when Skillet and we kids ran around in a hail storm with buckets on our heads?"

"Yes, you guys were bucket-heads. Remember the time the cat got into glue in his workshop, and Skillet picked her up. He came carrying her to the trailer because she was stuck to his hands. He couldn't open the door so he stood out there meowing for help. I had to cut her hair to get him loose. He chased me around the trailer with hair stuck to his hands. I liked to never got it all off of him."

"Yeah. Several of his fingers were glued together, too."

Weezie sat thoughtfully for a moment and then said, "Skillet weren't the kind to drop acid at a monster truck jam, and he never got arrested, but he sure was an ornery old SOB."

"Weezie, you swore. And what do you know about acid or monster trucks?"

"I just used a *sentence enhancer* is all. I watch COPS, and I still gets Skillet's Jacked-Up Trucks magazine." A pensive look followed. Her eyes watered. She said, "Skillet weren't ordinary, that's for sure."

We sat silently for a moment. My throat tightened as I fought back tears.

She asked, "Can you bring me a few of those plumes from that pampas grass you planted on your place?"

My throat clamped up so tight I couldn't swallow. Tears filled my eyes. "They're pink."

Weezie's face lit up. "Oh, I must have some." Another pause, and then she said, "Skillet's bad qualities were a gift."

"Yeah. A gift."

On Camping

He says I'm pretty as pork 'n beans
And hangs around, too long it seems
What part of no does he not understand?
He's not appealing, this kind of man

Front teeth gone, no happy ending
Meth and court dates must be pending
One single top tooth left to shine
A weird can opener comes to mind

In one case he could be a winner
If I were camping and needed dinner
But camping's not my cup of tea
And missing teeth so bother me

Chapter 7

We Were Warriors–Hell Bent

*Team Corbin: The potency of resolve,
the power of connectedness, and the force of love.*

I had never been good at anything medical. It took extreme fortitude just to get a flu shot or to give a blood sample. Yet there I was in a Neonatal Intensive Care Unit—a medical abyss —racked with fear. Somehow, I had to muster the strength to support my daughter and son-in-law as they faced a medical crisis with their newborn. I searched for a full measure of courage as my insides churned like waves against rocks. Little did I know I would soon become a warrior—hell bent.

I spotted my son-in-law in profile as I strode down the hall toward the Intensive Care Unit. A new father, he sat in a chair cupping his baby's head in his hands and talking to him softly. A baby bed labeled Baby Boy Corbin sat nearby. Nurses hovered. Wires dangled in all directions from the baby's body. Tiny feet peeked out from beneath a blue blanket. His head moved slightly from side to side as blinking eyes struggled to focus on a world foreign to him. The little guy would be in surgery soon. I imagined the words spoken by his rookie father—the promises made. "Daddy's here. We're in this together, buddy. I'll take care of you, no matter what. I promise. You can count on me."

Tears welled up in my eyes. I wiped them on my sleeve. Be strong, Grandma, be strong. You can do this. A nurse entered. Soon the baby wailed as needles jabbed at his tiny body.

* * *

My daughter, Mel, and son-in-law, Chris, learned that morning their baby was born with a serious condition. I was at their home preparing for the homecoming of the newborn when the phone rang. I knew immediately by my daughter's voice something was wrong. Her words stormed into me. "The baby is not okay." To this day, those words echo in my mind, replaying a chilling, defining moment that changed everything. "I'm sending Adrian to bring you to the hospital," she said. "Cole is scheduled for surgery as soon as the doctor gets here. I need you to come."

She could hardly talk. I asked no questions. "I'll be ready." When I arrived at Mel's hospital room, Chris had accompanied the baby to intensive care, and her best friend, Victoria, sat at her bedside. Adrian, Victoria's teenage son who drove me there, had dropped his mom off at the hospital before coming to pick me up. Victoria, under chemo treatments for breast cancer, required a driver. She was pale. A scarf covered her hairless head. This was her second fight with the disease. She shouldn't have been there, but nothing could keep her away.

I learned only a few details about the baby's life-threatening intestinal condition before a nurse entered with a wheelchair to escort us to Intensive Care. A sense of urgency prevailed. The baby would be whisked into surgery as soon as the operating team convened.

We marched urgently through the hospital halls and an underground tunnel to reunite with Chris and baby Cole in a nearby building. The air was tense as we traversed the long, narrow tunnel. The claustrophobic atmosphere, symbolic of my world at that moment, closed in on me. The nurse pushed a sobbing Mel as Victoria and I, wanting to be strong for her, tried to stifle tears. We couldn't.

The walk had to be hard on Victoria, but she kept up. I glanced over at her. Our eyes spoke—the message clear. She was in. I was in. I knew in that moment whatever it took to save this baby, we would do it. He was ours, and we were his. Team Corbin was born, and in that moment we became soldiers—hell bent.

Adrian marched along behind us. A teenage boy, he could have dropped his mother off and gone on to age-appropriate activities, but his demeanor showed the same fortitude his mother displayed. He was in. He hung with us all day. He and Mel had grown close over the years as she helped Vic raise her boys. He was there for Mel that day as well as for his mother—his presence a comfort to us all. Another soldier.

Nurse Debbie in intensive care was assigned to Baby Boy Corbin. She dropped hints of what to expect, no doubt preparing us for what was to come. This intestinal condition was often part of a syndrome which included kidney and heart issues, to name a few. After surgery, more tests would be required to determine the extent of complications. Debbie advised us, "Just take one step at a time. Don't borrow worries. Right now we've got to manage this surgery thing."

A rock, this woman stood between us and desperation. As the days progressed, we realized she not only cared for babies clinging to life, she nurtured parents searching for hope. Now, years later, we are grateful for the doctors who saved our baby—whose names we cannot recall—but it is Nurse Debbie we remember.

After several hours of hell in the surgery waiting room, the real battle began. Days were filled with a litany of tests, some of them painful. Cole's daddy stood by his side for every one. We were fortunate. No other conditions related to the dreaded syndrome were found. The intestinal issue was bad enough, though. It required considerable special care, three surgeries, and various treatments over the course of Cole's first year of life. The residual effects of those measures were unknown.

Team Corbin kicked in, and our individual aptitudes and skills complemented each other. Chris stayed at the hospital every night. He changed diapers, tended wounds, interacted with doctors, learned to read monitors, and understood the mechanics of every tube, wire, and machine.

His focus was fierce. I was with him in intensive care one day when Nurse Debbie became distracted with a crisis. She asked Chris to perform a procedure he had helped with before. It involved several tedious steps and sterilized supplies.

I watched him meticulously prepare for and execute the required care and helped where I could with a screaming, kicking baby. When we finished, the baby settled, and I sat down in a chair drained and sweaty. Chris stood there, looked around, and said, "I need to clean up my station." He gathered up wrappers, scraps of tape and gauze, and other refuse from the procedure, disinfected the countertop and his hands, organized "his station," set things up for the next treatment, and looked around for the next thing to do. I was wowed. I liked my son-in-law before this experience. I loved him when it was done.

Mel and I covered the day shift, at least as much as she could handle, so Chris could rest. Her primary role was defined by Cole's needs. He couldn't eat yet, but it was imperative he have breast milk when he could. A satisfactory prognosis depended on it. My primary job was to keep Mel fed, rested, and on schedule in the midst of chaos. Victoria, an always positive, can-do gal, took on the role of rallying friends, providing updates, and keeping Mel's hopes up. Adrian was available for transportation and errands.

* * *

When Cole finally got to go home from the hospital, Nurse Debbie and I watched Mel and Chris strap him into a carseat. Debbie said, "I see a lot of babies go home, and I worry about the care they'll get. I don't worry about Baby Boy Corbin." She was right about that. He had capable, devoted parents. And he had me, Grandma. I had no idea what that meant yet, but I was about to find out. This tiny creature, bundled in the protection of his carseat, was going to teach me lessons and enrich my world to a degree I could not have imagined. I would soon realize my greatest accomplishment. I would become the baby whisperer.

We had home health support and were able to savor the joys of a new baby, but the challenges were intimidating. Potential risks and future surgeries hovered like angry poltergeists. This was when Momma Mel kicked in. Her motive set, her focus clear, she became warrior mom.

She searched the Internet and found a support group. These online mothers of babies with the same condition as ours became part of Team Corbin. Determined to obtain the best possible care for her baby, Mel engaged in serious medical research and sought out renowned specialists around the country. After discovering innovative and cutting-edge procedures that were better than the ones Cole's doctor proposed, warrior mom got a new doctor and ran over her HMO like she was Desert Storm. She was, by god, going to fix her baby, and no one better get in her way. This included me. When I worried the intensity of her quest was upsetting her, she shut me down. I felt somewhat like her HMO.

She was right, though. The original treatment plan would not have produced an optimal outcome. There was a better way. To this day, when I look at the little guy (now eight years old), I think about what she did for him. Her tenacity and intervention changed his future.

Mel's struggle was not easy. I arrived for a visit one day to find the house in disarray. Letting housekeeping go was out of character for her. She lay on the sofa with Cole curled up next to her sleeping contentedly after breast feeding. She didn't greet me. I asked if she was okay. Without opening her eyes, she said, "I'm just taking care of my baby." It was clear, that was all she had in her. My role on Team Corbin kicked in. By three o'clock in the morning, the house was in order, and I slept with Cole resting on my chest.

Mel was desperate for rest. I stayed over many nights, nestled on the sofa with Cole sleeping on my chest so I could comfort him when he stirred. This stretched out the time between feedings. When I couldn't stall him off any longer, I delivered him to her bedside. After she fed him, I gathered him up for another episode of sleep. If necessary, I gently danced throughout the house while singing *I Love You a Bushel and a Peck*. Although exhausting, it was a blessed time. I learned that happiness is holding a sleeping baby.

Mel pushed an inconsolable, fussy Cole in my direction one day and said, "Can you do something with him? You're the baby whisperer." I knew then my purpose was clear, my mission set, and my role defined. The baby whisperer. I'll take that. I danced and sang that baby down with a soft Regge-esque lullaby.

Not long after that first surgery, I found a cement statue at a garden center of a father holding a newborn. The baby's head was cupped in his daddy's hands. The silhouette matched perfectly the profile I had seen as I walked down the hall of Intensive Care and spotted Chris holding Cole and making promises. I bought the statue, the price irrelevant. A treasure it was. I placed it on Mel and Chris's patio. When Cole was a toddler, he toppled it over and it broke. I was okay with that. I had bonded with the little guy in ways I could not have imagined, and that connection taught me what was really important.

* * *

After Cole's third and final surgery, we were in a hospital waiting for his body to deliver his first normal bowel movement. That result would determine the outcome of all our efforts. Once he pooped, we could take him home. We wanted poo. We needed poo. We must have poo. Day after day we waited for poo. Mel provided daily updates to a wide Internet group of concerned family, friends, and moms in the support group. Finally, one day she sent out the word, "We got poo. We're going home."

When we arrived home, a morphine induced state had Cole's eyes glazed over. A sheen of sweat shown on his face as his body fought to heal from wounds carved by a scalpel. As I rocked and patted gently, he transformed in my mind into something more than a baby. He became a creature of the universe, a being fighting to live. I wanted to will him to be well, to guarantee his future. I wished I could somehow transfer my life force to him, to make him whole. Even with the potency of those feelings, a peaceful contentedness prevailed within me. I felt such intense gratefulness for his existence that emotions welled up and took me over—their potency producing soft, polite tears. Butterflies fluttered in my stomach as he settled on my chest, his weight pressing against me. I wondered how he could sleep so contentedly with all that stirring in my core. Although salty tears made trails down my cheeks, a euphoric state took over as I held that vulnerable little soul fighting for his life. In that moment, I, the baby whisperer —a weeping, ordained warrior woman—felt more full and whole than ever in my life.

* * *

Cole is eight years old now. I call him my sidekick. Because of Team Corbin's efforts, he's a normal little guy, living life full out. To look at him, no one would guess the challenges of his beginning. He loves costumes, music, robots, and his computer. He has a younger sister whom he likes most of the time—sometimes not so much. She said to him one day "Cole, you don't have to tell me you love me."

He said, "I do love you. I just don't know it." Whatever that means, he has a sister, devoted parents, and Grandma GoGo. He is a lucky little guy. When I reminded him one day of how fortunate he was to have such wonderful parents, he responded, "Okay" and went on with his play. "I'm a lizard."

Mel occasionally delivers care packages to parents at the hospital who are going through what she and Chris experienced. Chris does volunteer search and rescue work, finding hikers lost on mountain hiking trails and delivering them to loved ones. He jumps out of helicopters, rappels down ravines, climbs rocky slopes, and trains diligently. Cole idolizes him, and well he should. Victoria beat the odds of her disease, had another baby, and runs her own business. Adrian, a grown man now, has a child of his own. And me, well, I'm retired and enjoying my second career as a writer.

Over the years, I've sat with my sidekick in cardboard boxes with flashlights, built couch cushion tents, and danced the Hokey Pokey. I've used a toy screwdriver to feed him macaroni and named meatballs after villains in cartoons to get him to eat. I've conducted chemistry experiments with Fruit Loops, shown him how to hide peas in a glass of milk, and served him marshmallows for dessert and told his mother he had fruit. I was a good disciplinarian, though. "Cole, don't run your toy tractor over your baby sister."

While at Victoria's house for lunch recently, Adrian and I had a chat. He said, "Every time I see Cole, I remember how the little guy's life began, and I look at him in wonder."

"I do the same," I said. "We saved him, you know."

"Yes, I know."

Cole is on the threshold of life. I'm on the tail end of mine. His newness, his rapidly developing mind, and his essence influence me in a way I find difficult to describe. It has something to do with the wonder of the universe and every creature in it. It has something to do with the connectedness of all living things. It has something to do with legacy. But mostly, it has something to do with a mysterious rustling inside of me when he and I sip chocolate milk through straws from a shared glass.

Some say love is about how people make each other feel. Cole makes me feel like just a part-time old person. Like I matter. Like I did something important. Like I can make a difference. Like I am relevant.

I wonder if Cole will ever know about Team Corbin. Will he know about his mother's fight that gave him the gift of normalcy? Will he know his father stood by him for tests and cared for him in intensive care? Will he know about the promises made while his soft newborn head was cupped in the palm of his father's hands? Will he know about the symbolic patio statue of a dad holding a baby—the one he toppled over? Will he know he slept on my chest night after night? Will he know about the tears I shed as I rocked his tiny body fighting to heal? Will he know about Victoria's sacrifices and Adrian's devotion? Will he know about Nurse Debbie? Will he know about Team Corbin, that we were warriors—hell bent?

Yes, someday, when he's older, he will know all these things. He will know them because his grandma is a writer.

Sidekick's Journey

Newborn, not perfect   nature's flaw
My grandson fights, just to *be*
His kin, stunned and resolute, are *in*
Our mission singleminded   our job assigned
We become warriors   hell bent

Scalpels, stitches, tubes
Morphine sweats, an infant's glazed eyes—
    unnatural but necessary
As the grandma, I comfort by day   gnash and wail by night
Silently, so no one sees the gaping, ragged wounds in my gut
Over and over, I rally, my focus renewed

My daughter, as the mother, gestates   still
Her role as creator haunts
Her pain is mine, her hell is mine, her resolve palpable
My world transforms into a tunnel   cradling the creature
I pray   a steely agnostic, yet I pray

Three years later   he's my sidekick. . . .perfect, almost
No, perfect
It is me who's flawed—delightfully so
I dance the Macarena   brilliantly, with flair
My sidekick determines, "My Grandma is c-a-r-a-a-z-y."

Chapter 8

A Date—Of Sorts

Thing 1 and Thing 2

Nothing prepared me for being a grandma. I observed the ridiculous behavior of friends as they achieved this status and concluded they were silly, perhaps even obnoxious. I saw my parents get goofy when I had children and thought they had lost their friggin' minds. I could not imagine my practical, pragmatic, fiercely independent, career-oriented self ever being that ridiculous. Then came Baby Boy Cole.

He was six-month-old when I had plans to fly from Oklahoma to California to see him. I couldn't wait, and was telling a friend at work what I was going to do to him when I got my hands on him. "I'm going to chew on his thighs and blow on his tummy."

A man passing by overheard the comment and asked, "Nikki, you got a date?"

"Yes, and I'm in love."

Cole is eight now. We go on dates, usually for his preferred food, Won Ton soup at Pink Chop Sticks. The servers there know us and are clear on the fact Cole is the man in charge of seating, ordering, issuing pleases and thank you's, and handing over my credit card. Putting my sidekick in charge transforms his behavior from one of a hyped-up orangutan informing me of the color of gum under the table to an in-charge little Mr. Man. He takes his role seriously.

Sometimes his sister comes along, which changes the dynamics. I call her my girlfriend. When I dropped her off at pre-school one day the teacher asked her if I was her grandma. She said, "No, she's my girlfriend."

I call Cole my sidekick. Sometimes those names don't apply and I call them Thing 1 and Thing 2, which captures their spirits perfectly. If they are both present, we have futile conversations in the car before entering an establishment wherein I remind them, "Don't act normal."

This is necessary because everything is more challenging when both of them tag along. The dynamics are similar to the behavior of dogs. If you have one dog, it's like having another person. If you have two dogs, it's like having two dogs. When you have two children in a restaurant, at some point they are going to use the table as a tent.

In general, food is only a slight diversion, but shish kabobs delivered with a flaming pot can introduce enough novelty and danger to distract The Things from outrageous, ill-mannered tendencies, at least for about five minutes.

I learned years ago not to get into a fight with a four-year-old, so I rarely included my grandchildren in eating out experiences unless they involved a playground. The Pink Chop Sticks changed that. It is a place for conversation, and I take full advantage of this opportunity to instill core values and to reinforce a theme I promote as often as possible—that these children are privileged and fortunate, something they would not know if I didn't tell them.

"You might have the most wonderful parents ever."

"Is a bug bomb strong enough to kill lizards and tigers?" Cole asks.

"I don't know. Maybe."

"Little spiders turn into big spiders," his sister advises with a lisp through missing front teeth.

You know, not every kid is fortunate enough to have season tickets to Disneyland," I say.

Cole, who dresses as a Mary Poppins' chimney sweep and is often swept into the Disneyland parade, asks, "Am I famous?"

"Yes. Sort of."

"Can we go to Target? I want an Incredible Hulk hammer."

"You can't have anything with which you might injure your sister."

"I won't pound her with it."

I may be Grandma GoGo—an old softy—but I'm not an idiot. There is a reason all the toy swords in Cole's house are stashed behind the headboard of my bed in the guest room. No doubt he planned to pound his sister. "That's what you said last time I bought you a weapon. Pick something else."

To get in on the act, his sister says, "I want a...a...a...something."

Cole seeks confirmation. "So, we can go to Target?"

"Sure." In California, I have no life, except as the role of Grandma GoGo, and toys are often on the agenda because I am the toy fairy. "Cole, eat your rice. It's not okay to put won tons on your napkin. Here's a plate."

"I'm a zombie."

Little bumpkins pick dumplings, shrimp, and veggies out of Won Ton soup before eating what's left, which is little else. A dual barfing episode materializes when one of them touches a mushroom. In spite of this exception, good manners are on full display—a requirement for the toy store visit. Burps are followed with "excuse me's" and, if any farts occur, accidentally, of course, we all agree the culprit stepped on a duck.

Chapter 9

In Praise of Men In Uniforms

Oh, to be rescued.

Thing 1 and Thing 2 were coming for a visit, which required preparations: meds relocated, furniture turned into blockades, glass tabletop corners cushioned, and an alarm set on balcony doors so a *ding, ding, ding* signals when orders are ignored not to pet Coco (a squirrel who begs for food). And, carseats must be installed.

This last task seemed simple enough, but I watched my son-in-law perform this function one day and concluded for me it would be a physical, mental, and mechanical challenge equivalent to overhauling a motor. But, as Grandma GoGo, a woman determined to assure the safety of precious, pug-nosed, pudgy-legged little criminals, I embraced my I am woman watch me roar mentality and prepared for the task. This meant eating all the bacon I wanted and mustering the courage and determination to, by god, install carseats.

I dug them out of the tornado shelter stuffed so full that if I had to get in there, something would have to come out. Intimidating belts and hooks dangled from the seats, suggesting menacing mechanical requirements—not my forte. Perplexing instruction manuals did nothing to mitigate my interpretation of the situation. In spite of the gloomy prospects, I made a good go of it. No sentence enhancers were used in the process in spite of a level of frustration equal to parallel parking.

These efforts failed, and reality prevailed. No amount of bacon would equip GoGo for the challenge of properly installing carseats. So off I went to Fire Station 4.

Under the impression from a news report that firemen would check out carseat installations as a civic duty, I pulled up in front of Station 4. Men in uniforms—navy t-shirts with gold emblems and matching pants—crawled like ants over a red firetruck, polishing and pampering. Bruce Springsteen blasted from some source, and the energy of the young, fit men was palpable. As I approached, several of them looked at me curiously. They must have wondered what this old lady was up to. A young hunk asked, "Can we help you?"

I put on my best and well-practiced begging and pleading routine. "I'm old, please help me. My grandchildren are arriving at the airport today and I have a dilemma. I'm picking them up, and I can't get these damn carseats installed. I've been told you fellows check out carseat installations. Clearly I have failed. Can you help me?"

"I'm sorry, ma'am. We only do that on certain days and at another station."

I looked pathetic. Desperate. Downtrodden. "Oh my, what shall I do? They're arriving in a few hours."

An attractive young man dropped from the top of the firetruck and approached, "I've got kids. I'm a carseat aficionado. Let's take a look."

In a matter of seconds, four gorgeous, uniformed man-butts protruded from the four doors of my car as they wrestled carseats into proper positions and secured them so tightly they would not budge a millimeter under any circumstances. "That should do it, ma'am."

"Indeed."

I wanted to hug all of them, or perhaps ravage them, but I exercised extreme self-discipline, thanked them profusely, and went on my way. As I pulled out of the driveway, the vision in the rear view mirror of Tulsa's finest mounting the firetruck to resume their duties grabbed my attention at which time I concluded I had been blessed with a near-sex experience extraordinaire.

After Thing 1 and Thing 2 left a week later, I realized the carseats were so solidly installed there was no way I could de-install them. Oh darn. Off I went to Fire Station 4.

A Man in Uniform

Oh, hi.

Chapter 10

Rich Man's Sport

Waves of Loss and Love

Dust billows behind brawny trucks decorated with logos and pulling showy, oversized trailers loaded with horses and howling dogs. Chance sits on the front steps of the bunkhouse, rubbing the stubble from his first shave and observing the procession rumbling down the ranch road. Wealthy men drive the trucks. Fussy, blond women in fancy boots and jeans decorated with sparkles ride shotgun. Chance doesn't care for such women. They remind him of those he meets when he visits his mother in Tulsa—women with long, polished fingernails who drink wine and wear jewelry to swimming pools.

Blue chases the trailers. No amount of scolding stops her. Dad won't let Chance shut her in the bunkhouse, so he gives up on discipline and allows her to run back and forth between the bunkhouse and the ranch clubhouse where the hunt is being staged. Because of the trucks, the horses, and the dogs, she goes nuts during hunt days.

Blue was a puppy when the ranch's owner gave her to Chance after his mom left. Purebred Blue Heelers were valuable, so he understood she was special right off.

Sometimes he sleeps with her outside in the bed of Dad's old Ford truck or in a sleeping bag in the yard. It is there Chance worships stars, like real cowboys did years ago on cattle drives, and hopes ticks have a preference for herding dogs.

Chance disapproves of the rich man's hunt. They invade the ranch on weekends and gallop through pastures on purebred horses pursuing bellowing hounds on the trail of newly released coyotes. These wealthy men rate this sport on the level of a fox hunt. Chance considers it a joke. He likes the hounds, though, and loves romping with them.

His dad slams the screen door, whacks Chance playfully on the back of the head, and strides cowboy-like toward the ranch clubhouse, swinging a sack of mountain oysters. The ranch hands will fry them up for lunch and attempt to convince naive guests the testicles are chicken nuggets.

Later, as Chance munches on breakfast cereal, he spots Blue out of the kitchen window, nipping at the heels of a bull in the pasture. Roscoe is disinterested. He's king of the world, and he knows it. *Good luck, Blue.* Although only a year old, Blue has proven to be a good herder. She herded a bunch of partiers on the patio at the main ranch house. She bumped up against whoever stood most apart from the crowd. Once that person moved in, she chose the next candidate. When she had everyone crowded into a corner of the patio, the revelers noticed they had been herded. Fascinated, they spread back out and watched as Blue diligently herded them again. Her performance was great party entertainment, which made Chance as proud as a dad whose kid had hit a home run.

Although that is a Blue success story, the prospect of Blue rounding up Roscoe is slim. *I hope Roscoe doesn't take you seriously and kick you in the head.*

Later, Chance heads to the clubhouse to help his dad prepare lunch for the hunters. He gets paid for helping out. Blue is nowhere to be seen. Chance observes riders sweep past Roscoe in the south pasture led by baying hounds hot after their prey. As he approaches the clubhouse, he notices one of the fancy women making a gallant effort to corral a litter of tiny puppies running amuck. "Can I hold one?" he asks.

"Sure." The lady picks up the runt of the litter. "His name is Biscuit."

The pup licks and nuzzles, wags and wiggles. Chance doesn't want to give him up, but his dad needs help with lunch, so he hands Biscuit back.

The lady smiles and reaches out to shake his hand. No woman has ever done that before. He awkwardly takes it and thanks her, calling her "ma'am" as his father, a gentleman cowboy, taught him.

Not long after, he is in the clubhouse stuffing bottles of Mexican beer into a tub of ice. His dad comes in. Two ranch hands trail behind but stop just inside the door.

"Son," he says, putting his hand on Chance's shoulder, "Blue is gone."

"What do you mean *gone?*"

"The hounds lost the coyote's trail. Blue was in the area. She ran, and they zeroed in on her. She's gone, Buddy."

Chance glances at the ranch hands who shade their eyes behind brims of cowboy hats and shift their weight from side to side. Dad pats Chance's shoulder and heads back outside, his head low and his stride lacking its usual energetic gait. The ranch hands tip their hats and follow. Chance stares for a moment at the empty space they leave before he resumes cramming beer into the ice-filled tub. A tear drops onto his hand. *Those goddamned rich people and their sonsabitchen, stupid-ass dogs.*

Chance struggles through the day, setting up tables and chairs and helping serve food. Afterward, he's cleaning up when his dad approaches.

"Go home, son. We'll take it from here."

Ranch hands watch as Chance slinks away. Rich people lower their heads. Some look away.

After slamming the front door and marching to his room, Chance flings himself on his bed and sobs. He remembers how Blue would bound onto the bed to comfort him when he felt bad. She would circle around, nudge him, lick his face, and plunk down next to him, her breath on his face and the pressure of her chin on his shoulder. He would pull her close, aware of the softness of her coat and the warmth of her body. *Oh, god, she's gone. My Blue is gone. Oh, god.*

It is late afternoon when Dad comes home, carrying containers of leftovers. He wakes Chance from a fitful sleep. "This may sound strange, Buddy, but the dog owners want to give you a puppy. I'll understand if you don't want that. It's little consolation and probably too soon, but the offer was made."

Chance's throat tightens. He can hardly breathe. His voice is scratchy. "I don't want it."

"Probably a good call." His dad pats him on the thigh and leaves. Chance hears the rich men's trucks rumble down the road—their dogs howling—and presses a pillow over his head.

* * *

Several months later, Chance helps with a hunt for the first time since he lost Blue. Back home afterward, he helps his dad load the freezer with leftovers. Someone knocks at the door, and the woman who shook his hand enters holding a dog. Chance does not move. He cannot move. She holds the pup out to him. "It's Biscuit," she said. "He's my favorite. I saved him for you."

The pup squirms and stretches out to Chance, kicking furiously, trying to free himself from her grasp. Chance still can't move. The lady puts the dog down. He circles Chance, jumping up and begging for a pick up. Chance looks at the lady. Her eyes are misty. He looks at his dad, who is also misty-eyed. Biscuit is going nuts. Finally, Chance picks him up. "He's pretty healthy for being the runt," he says.

"He's a good dog, and he has your name written all over him," Dad says.

Biscuit wags his tail frantically, licks Chance's face, and bites at his ear. He burrows his nose into Chance's neck briefly, sneezes, and explores the rest of his face. Biscuit's whole body is churning. The dog is beside himself. Chance laughs, which increases Biscuit's excitement. "Yep. I'll take him."

"He's yours," the lady says and reaches out her hand for a handshake.

Excitement churns in Chance's stomach. "Thank you, ma'am."

"Would you like to stay for supper?" Dad asks the lady.

"Sure. I'll help." She and Dad head to the kitchen.

The screen door slams as Chance heads outside to romp with Biscuit. *Maybe rich people aren't so bad after all.*

Chapter 11

Raccoons Need Love, Too

Punked by a wild, masked jokester.

Large, closely-connected families on both my father and mother's sides were a major part of my life while growing up on a farm in Iowa. Most of them lived near us on farms outside of a small rural community. This provided rich opportunities for interaction with grandparents, aunts, uncles, cousins . . . and animals.

Uncle Fred had a pet raccoon, Howie. His kids rescued him as an orphan, and he became a beloved pet. Once raised, Howie became a radical nuisance by any definition. He established his residence in one of the outbuildings on the farm. When someone headed in that direction, he ran to a hole in the back wall, climbed onto the rafters, and jumped down on them when they entered.

This was an unfathomable shock to anyone experiencing it. Uncle Fred thought it hilarious, though. He enticed unsuspecting souls to go into the building for some reason, then waited anxiously to observe the attack. Howie's victims would think they were going to retrieve a basket of peaches and, instead, they'd end up punked from above by a wild, masked jokester. After this unimaginable fright, they stumbled out of the building waving their hands as though they had walked into a spider web.

* * *

Cousin Mary recently moved to Arkansas and had converted to the Southern Baptist religion. This inspired her to take on the mission of converting her Methodist relatives in the interest of saving their souls from eternal damnation. The probability of converting Iowa Methodists into Baptists was an unlikely proposition, but she never gave up on the prospect of convincing morally bankrupt relatives of their sinful ways.

If cousin Mary had been present at the instant Howie dropped from the rafters onto an unsuspecting victim, she might have been able to wring a successful conversion out of a determined Methodist.

At a family dinner at Uncle Fred's farm, relatives gathered in the expansive front yard for grace before a meal. Howie, sat at Fred's feet as family members of all ages stood in a circle hand-in-hand, heads bowed. Cousin Mary, remaining hopeful against all odds, gave a long and enthusiastic blessing as restless children fidgeted and adults courteously posed as reverent enthusiasts.

A cat joined the prayer group, moving around the circle brushing up against people's legs as cats do. This caught the attention of the participants, at least those with their eyes open, and the restless children. When she got near Howie, he reached out, grabbed her and proceeded to hunch her.

A terrible racket ensued. The kids' eyes got big, and adults looked on in horror. Cousin Mary, being vested in her determination to save us heathens, didn't miss a beat in her prayer but abandoned bowing her head and began praying to the heavens.

Uncle Fred ended the fiasco by kicking Howie—hard. He tumbled into the middle of the circle, got up, shook his body, and crippled off with a gait that included a strange sideways motion. The cat slunk away in the opposite direction, reeling from the near-sex experience.

Cousin Mary saved no souls that day.

The Not So Great Outdoors

Most people love the great out yonder
They hike, and climb, and stare in wonder
They worship rivers, falls, and peaks
Splendid scenes they aim to seek

I see rocks and sticks and dirt
Scratches, bites, and endless hurt
Snakes and spiders, bugs, and bears
Poison plants and clothing tears

Monster boulders often falling
Varmints lurking, coyotes calling
What's wrong that I cannot see
The magic of nature's mystery

I ponder deep and soon I know
The reason I am feeling so
Camping is Las Vegas worthy
After two days, I feel dirty

Chapter 12

The Rally

The Audacity of Possibilities

Jade felt like an old horse dropped off at the glue factory. Her man had left her for a woman twenty years her junior. Bodie met his new love at a fitness center. It only took the gal a couple of months to land him. Jade learned about Bodie's girlfriend when the gal called the house. "Is this Jade Conrad?"

"Yes."

"My name's Earleen and I have something you need to know. Bodie and I are in love. I'm the kinda woman who gets to the heart of a matter, so I wanted you ta know. Bodie told me ya'all wasn't happy together, and I think it's best for all of us if you let him go."

Jade froze. She couldn't speak. Earleen prattled on. "You need to understand Bodie and I really do love each other."

Jade still couldn't speak.

"Hello. Hello. I'm not the kinda woman to break folks up, but your relationship has gone stale, you know, and Bodie needs to be set free so he can find happiness."

Silence.

"I really am a nice person, and me and my kids need someone to take care of us. Bodie and I have lots in common with our interest in fitness and all. I'm not the kinda woman to cause any trouble ordinarily, but if you was to let him go, we could all be happy. He don't want to stay with you, but he feels bad, and it's hard for him to tell you that. So I wanted— "

Something stirred in Jade, a blend of hate and horror. This silly woman, whoever she was, had to be delusional. Bodie would never do anything like that, and he certainly wouldn't be attracted to such a simple-minded woman. "I don't give a flying fuck what kinda woman you are. Don't you ever call here again." Jade hung up the phone and dropped it on a sofa cushion as though it were a hot rock.

The phone rang again. Jade stared at it. *The nerve of that woman.* No way would she answer. She tried to wrap her mind around what had just happened when she heard Bodie's car in the driveway. He entered the house whistling, dropped his workout bag on the counter, and kissed Jade on the cheek. Jabbering about his day, he headed to the bedroom, stripping off workout clothes on the way.

A cloud swirled in Jade's head, and a grinding hurt raged. Not one to nestle comfortably into a state of denial, it didn't take her but a few minutes to digest the meaning of the disgusting phone call. When Bodie returned Jade had entered the kitchen out of habit with the intent of fixing dinner. But all she could do was brace herself against the kitchen counter. His entrance forced the fogginess out of her head. Bodie picked up the evening paper and announced, "I need to go to Chicago Thursday and will be there through the weekend. I've got to tie down some details on one of our suppliers there. I'll be home late Sunday night."

"Is Earleen going along?" Jade asked.

Bodie's face faded to an ashen shade so quickly he looked like he would faint. It took him a minute to speak. "How did you know?"

"Your ridiculous girlfriend, Earleen, called. She told me she was the kinda woman who gets to the heart of a matter, that you love her, not me, and I should let you go."

"Oh my god, let me explain."

"There's no explaining that away. According to Earleen you need a workout partner, so I'm giving you to her as a present. It's called revenge." Jade threw the dishtowel she was holding down on the counter and marched to the bedroom. Once there, she had no idea how she felt or what to do. The shock was so deep she paced vigorously, swinging her arms to match the broad steps. *I should cry, but I can't. I don't even want to.* She didn't know what to do. Her insides churned.

Bodie came in and tried to hug her, but she pushed him away. "Get out!" she said. He did. And it was over, just like that.

* * *

Jade called her best friend, Blaze, who came right over. They talked for hours while Jade cried. The impertinence of Earleen's intrusion into her and Bodie's relationship, as rusty as it was, nudged both women into a state of loathing.

Jade dabbed a tissue to her eyes. "I can imagine him telling Earleen, 'She kicked me out for no reason at all.' I'm actually okay with that. It's a relief to have his somber, despondent presence out of the house. I do feel a tad like a member of The First Wives Club, though."

"Did you not see this coming?" Blaze asked.

"Not really, but looking back I realize I should have. He's been working out a lot, and the vitality in his voice lately is in stark contrast to his normal gloomy disposition. Now that I think about it, he has been uncharacteristically vibrant. And he's been spending a lot of chatroom time on the computer, sometimes in the middle of the night. Texting activity has increased as well. I blamed it all on work."

Understanding now what was driving Bodie's out-of-character exuberance erased any of Jade's doubts about the blooming romance. She had lost her man to another woman.

"So you kicked him out?" Blaze asked.

"Yeah. I mean something broke inside of me. Thinking of him wanting someone else is disgusting, and his foolishness at wanting someone like that dimwitted, mentally-challenged fool is repulsive. Even the prospect of an emotional betrayal is a game changer for me, and there is no doubt their relationship has gone way beyond that. According to Earleen, they're practically engaged." Jade's throat tightened. Her stomach churned. Her ten-year relationship with Bodie was over. The question was: Did she care?

* * *

Bodie came by the next day. Although contrite and pleading for understanding, he made no effort to redeem the situation. There was no, "I'm sorry," and he showed no empathy for Jade. Instead, he focused on explaining and smoothing things over. Jade believed he did so to feel better about himself. When that didn't work and he realized the extent of her anger, he said, "Now, I don't want you causing trouble for Earleen."

Jade bristled. *Oh, no, he didn't.* Stunned by the swift and total shift of loyalty, her anger could not be contained, and she went medieval on Bodie. She bellied up to him. Her voice boomed, and she poked his chest with her finger. "I have no interest in having anything to do with E-a-r-l-e-e-n. EVER. Did it not occur to you she is causing trouble for me? She knows about me, so she is an interloper. This means she's either a nice person who is desperate, or she is not a nice person, which suggests a character flaw. Either way, you lose. You have to deal with that. I don't."

Bodie's head wobbled like a bobblehead toy. Jade suspected he couldn't deal with bad words being said about Earleen. She was about to kick him out again when curiosity got the best of her. And he seemed in no hurry to go. The tattered remains of friendship surfaced. She offered him coffee, and they settled in at the familiar kitchen counter where many years of conversations had taken place. Picking up on the extreme immaturity revealed by Earleen's "I'm the kinda woman" narrative, Jade asked, "How old is Earleen?"

"Thirty-two."

"Really? You went that low? How many children?"

"Two."

"Really?"

"Does she have fake boobs?"

"Now wait a minute. . ."

"Does she?"

"Well yeah."

"Really? Have you considered that Earleen, 'the kinda woman who gets to the heart of a matter,' has a symbiotic relationship with stupidity?" Bodie fidgeted and gave Jade a piercing look she had never seen before, one that incorporated a blatant display of arrogance. Jade guessed Bodie was defensive because he knew he had traded down. He needed to convince her he made a good decision so he could feel better about his actions. As strange as it seemed, he cared what Jade thought, and it frustrated him to hear her put Earleen down. He sat up straight in his chair. His lips tightened as he glared at her. She glared back with equal indignation.

Although Earleen owned him now, Jade had a hold on Bodie, and she could read him. "What is it about Earleen that made it so easy for you to risk what we had?" Jade asked. *Let me get details and torture myself as much as possible.*

She learned Earleen had been scammed by a man she'd gotten engaged to on the Internet without ever having met him. She had also been married several times and had two kids by two different men. Neither one of them married her. She couldn't keep a job, was living on food stamps, had rented furniture, and had accumulated substantial debt. Jade suspected Bodie was hankering to rescue Earleen from heartbreak, maxed-out credit cards, and a life plagued with victimization. The depth of his desperation to do so was impressive. In contrast, he had no opportunity to rescue Jade, a successful, independent woman.

Jade concluded, in addition to Earleen's immaturity, her judgement was off. Desperate and ripe for rescue, she hit the jackpot with Bodie. Jade wondered what the woman offered Bodie other than her mess. *Must be the boobs.* Although Jade didn't interpret this as Bodie trading up, she couldn't help but feel humiliated. How could such a woman take her man so easily? *Wasn't Bodie better than that? Surely he was not that stupid.* He was.

"Does it not bother you that this woman is willing to get involved with you while you are in a committed relationship with someone else?" Jade asked.

Bodie stared at her. Finally, he said, "I think you would like her if you got to know her."

The intensity of Jade's response to that suggestion was out of character. Slowly, emphatically, and leaning in till nose-to-nose with Bodie she commanded, "You keep. . .that woman. . .away from me." Her eyes flared and her chin shook as she spoke. Bodie leaned back in his chair and stared.

After packing up a few things, he hugged Jade goodbye. Closing the door behind him, her throat tightened and tears streamed down her face. She called Blaze. "I'm glad Bodie is gone, but I'm going to hurt over his leaving for a long time."

"I know," Blaze said, "It's the attachment, you know. We get attached to people, and even when it's not working anymore, breaking that attachment is hard."

"You know what's maddening? He just wants me out of the way so he can have someone else. It's so easy for him to give 'us' up. I don't think he hurts at all while I feel as though he reached into my stomach and ripped my guts out, leaving a gaping hole with bleeding tentacles dangling about. That sounds gross, but that's how wounded I am. Intellectually, I know my life will be better without him and his grumpy temperament, but the loss is hurtful. And scary. In spite of our differences, I still love him."

"You stayed because of that love, even when it faded," Blaze counseled. "He rewarded your loyalty by cheating and rejecting you for a bimbo, a woman who cannot possibly be a step up. The bizarre thing is he always said he didn't want to have children. I'm here to tell you, he'll regret this decision someday. I'm betting, at some point, he'll beg you to take him back."

"He probably will, but that's not going to happen."

* * *

Jade and Bodie quickly sold their house and divided up property. They did so without conflict. As they negotiated details, Jade took advantage of the tiny bit of guilt that played on Bodie's conscience. Excited about his new life, he had become uncharacteristically upbeat about everything and showed considerable benevolence toward Jade. As his disposition improved, his energy level amped up. She described it to Blaze this way, "Earleen is his Zoloft and his Red Bull. He's on fire."

During this process, Earleen made efforts to agitate. Her *I wants* got the better of her as Jade and Bodie divided things up, and she hankered for drama. Bodie was having none of her interference, though.

Once the mechanics of the separation were complete, Jade was ready to be done with the whole thing. But over the next few months, Bodie and Earleen frequently showed up at places where they knew she would be—the same restaurants and entertainment venues Bodie and Jade had frequented, even the same grocery store. This irritated Jade. Bodie had bought a house in another part of town, and she saw no reason for them to drive across town to hang out in her territory.

She suspected Earleen was behind these coincidences and Bodie was being manipulated. This was confirmed when she entered the sanctuary of her church one Sunday to discover Bodie and Earleen sitting in the pew Jade had sat in for years. His arm was around Earleen, and she pressed up tight against him. Bodie rarely went to church. Astounded, Jade turned around and went back into the foyer to pull herself together. *What to do?* Then an idea came to her.

She marched down the aisle, nestled in close to Bodie and gave him a lingering hug, during which she stared into Earleen's eyes. He lit up like an all-night casino when he saw her and hugged her back. She knew he would. Ignoring Earleen, she reeled Bodie into a conversation and kept it going until the service started. She even shared a hymn book with him during one of the songs. In the foyer after the service, she hugged Bodie goodbye then reached over, shook Earleen's hand, and whispered in her ear, "Good luck with that." Jade squeezed Bodie's hand as she turned to walked away. He grinned. Earleen's puzzled expression said, "How did that just happen?"

Jade couldn't wait to get on the phone and tell Blaze what happened. "Can you believe they did that? The unmitigated gall."

"People are basically rude and inconsiderate," Blaze suggested. "It was Earleen's idea. Bodie would never instigate such a thing. I'm sure he paid royally for how this turned out."

Jade agreed. "I bet they don't show up at church again. Earleen's hair was ratted up so high there could be a cell phone in there, and she flaunted embarrassingly profound cleavage. I'm guessing she's 'the kinda woman' who thinks wrapping herself in Saran Wrap is sexy, missing the implication that it suggests leftovers." The girls giggled. "I had no trouble sucking Bodie in. I think he misses me. I miss him, too. If I wanted to, I could engage him in a friendship relationship, you know, call him at work every day, chat him up, and ask him to lunch. He would participate. With all kinds of opportunities to insert myself into their lives, I could drive Earleen mad."

"No doubt you could deliver considerable payback, but you need to move on."

"You're right. My feelings are still tender, but I know I do not want Bodie back. It was a good run, but it's over."

"What you need, girlfriend, is a new boyfriend."

"I don't think so. This has left me wounded. I have trust issues. I doubt I will ever love again."

* * *

"Get dressed. We're going out," Blaze said.

"I'm not in the mood," Jade responded.

"Aw, come on. You've cocooned long enough. It's time to get back into the swing of things."

Blaze was a determined woman. When she decided on something, it was going to happen. Over the years the women had nursed each other through numerous crises, large and small. Blaze was the spark that lit Jade up. It had been several months since the breakup, and Blaze's solution to any problem was fun. So over the next few months they went out together, most frequently to a Tulsa country dance hall. A community atmosphere existed among the regulars there. In that playful venue, Jade was distracted from her wounds. She came alive. She had fun.

Having grown up on a farm, Jade harbored a fondness for country boys in spite of her metropolitan lifestyle. To her, nothing was more gleeful than a two-stepping cowboy steering her through a crowded dance floor as if he were a fine quarter horse working cattle.

Blaze met Travis during one of their outings. As a homicide investigator, he displayed the good-old-boy persona common to professions conducive to male bonding. Although he possessed a risk-taking temperament, Travis exuded a level of common sense and sophistication not normally attributed to the breed. And the cynical, detached edge so common to men who have seen too much of the underbelly of society was softened by an eccentric sense of humor everyone who knew him relished.

His passion and enthusiasm for what he did was appealing to Blaze. She had served in the military, so she displayed the same hard edges and strong sense of duty as Travis. This made them compatible. She relished the excitement and drama his job entailed and easily adjusted to the strange hours he worked.

Jade developed an easy friendship with Travis, and he often accompanied the girls on their forays to the dance hall. He tried repeatedly to persuade her to go out with his friend, Tucker. But Jade—no longer open to romantic possibilities—was having none of it.

* * *

After just a few months of dating, Travis proposed to Blaze, and she accepted. Her priorities shifted quickly. Planning a wedding and taking up housekeeping was a huge distraction. Jade was happy for her friend, but both women had become so anti-relationship oriented she puzzled over Blaze's new willingness to commit to marriage. "You said you'd never marry again. What changed your mind?" she asked Blaze.

"Remember how it irritated my ex when I sniffled from allergies? Well, the morning after our first night together Travis and I both sniffled all the way through breakfast. I took it as a sign. And he lets me be me. I don't have to lie and say I had a salad when I ate pizza like I did with my controlling ex. Travis goes to chick-flick movies with me without complaint. We even cook together. He's teaching me how to prepare kale. I thought the way to do that was to throw it out and fry bacon. I'm so happy, I'd sing to him except I love him too much."

"Do you realize how rare your relationship is? I think maybe you won the lottery with this one."

"I feel cherished. I've never felt that before."

"Hmmm. I don't think I have either. I like that. I suspect the odds of that happening for me are slim. And I sure don't want another gloomy man. Any man I'd be interested in would have to have shiny, sparkly eyes."

"Sounds good."

"You and Travis have only known each other a few months. Don't you think you should put some more time in on this relationship before committing?"

"No. I'm good. He's the one. You know how I know? He said he'd fight a bear for me. Not a grizzly bear or one of those black bears, but, you know, one of those Care Bears."

"Ha. Have you washed his truck yet?"

"No. But last weekend, he washed my car, gassed it up, checked the oil and tire pressure, charged my phone, and played me a Pink Floyd love song on his guitar."

"There is no such thing as a Pink Floyd love song."

"Maybe it was Phish, then."

"You're a mess. I support whatever you decide. I'm going to miss my run-around buddy, though. I'm missing you already. Things will never be the same."

"We'll always be friends, but you're right. After the wedding, the prowling days will be over. I know that for you this will be another loss. I worry about you, but there's a sureness about you that was not there before. Bodie did you a favor with his betrayal."

"I know. I've adjusted, and I'm glad it happened. I just wish it had happened differently. Forgiveness has settled in, though. I rarely think about him, and when I do, I don't have any feelings. It's not a void, but rather a neutral thing. I bet neither one of them work out anymore, and the kids are probably driving Bodie insane. I imagine her 'as the kinda woman' who begs to go out while Bodie, burrowed into his recliner and smoking a cigar, watches *Bonanza*. Maybe not. Maybe he's better to her than he was to me. If so, good for her. I'm just glad it's not me."

"How do you know when you've reached the point of forgiveness?" Blaze asked.

"When it doesn't hurt anymore. When you can say his name and feel nothing. When you wish the other parties well, and hope it works out for the kids' sake."

The serenity in Jade's voice comforted Blaze. She looked her friend in the eyes long and hard and then smiled as she took a sip of coffee. "I think we girls should have one last single-girl hurrah at the dance hall before the wedding."

* * *

"Would you like to dance, darlin'?" someone asked. Jade was a sucker for a man who called her darlin'. She turned around to discover a vision of cowboy glory—black hat, Wrangler jeans, tailored pearl-snap shirt, and a leather belt studded with silver. A gleaming oversized belt buckle finished off the look. The cowboy was fine.

On the way to the dance floor, Jade got a whiff of Stetson aftershave. As they danced, she noticed the guy's shiny, sparkly eyes. Possibilities. The cowboy finished Jade off as he navigated the crowded dance floor like a fine quarter horse working cattle. Blaze watched and smiled.

"What's your name?" he asked.

"Jade."

He grinned. "Nice to meet you, Jade. My name is Tucker."

A Bee Gees Frame of Mind

A polite rain falls on the windshield
As I consider if my heart has healed
Emotions lay dormant for so long
Now no feelings stir from a Bee Gees Song

I saw them there all full of cheer
Her glittery dress like a chandelier
A fancy fur of unknown origin
A designer dress she looked good in

I lived in a world of discontent
When I was his before he went
Today I'm whole, full, complete
With her, there's no need to compete

I gave him to her as a present
Living with him was not pleasant
Revenge the motive because they cheated
Rage my master for things he did

Her back was turned when our eyes met
I could see his discontent
I knew him well and I could tell
Regret festered in his hell

If eyes could talk, his would say
"I should have never gone away."
If mine could speak, I would lament,
"I'm sorry for your discontent."

How do you know forgiveness harkens?
When you say his name and nothing hardens?
I ponder deep and then I know
I forgave him long ago

Feelings floundered there between us—
Shades of emotions tender yet callous
How do you know when love is gone?
When no feelings stir from a Bee Gees song.

Chapter 13

Transvaginal Ultrasound, The Thumper, and Anthrax

Medical Madness

It was Dr. Willard's first day at work as the company's new medical director. "I need a 600 mg prescription for Demerol for a bladder infection," I said.

I considered it part of my job to haze new medical directors, lest their God complex ran rampant. A corporate executive making a request for a controlled substance from a company's medical director on his first day did the hazing job nicely. It provoked panic unusual for a medical professional, except in the case of Dr. Willard, who had my number.

"We can do that," he said. "Take your clothes off. I'll need to do an exam."

"Touché."

Dr. Willard's office was next to mine. He and I worked on many projects together over the years and developed a close professional relationship. And I benefited personally from having a doctor next door. He became my first point of contact when medical conditions surfaced,

We engaged in friendly banter, often of the irreverent sort. Dr Willard suggested the best approach to contraception was a gun in the bedside stand. When I engaged him in a conversation about the controversial topic of transvaginal ultrasounds, he responded, "I'm not up on rock bands." He said, "If you lost fifteen pounds you could increase your end-of-life stint in Harjoe's Nursing Home and Tattoo Parlor by three months." He also advised me that if I stopped eating bacon, my biological age would exceed my chronological one, and I could live long enough to become a wise and wrinkled old Obi Wan Kanobi.

In spite of such harassment, Dr. Willard was a valuable resource for medical advice. If I had not lost access to him after retirement, I could have avoided some medical traumas.

For example: I complained to my primary care doctor that my back ached around my left shoulder blade after which I found myself in a cardiologist's office that afternoon. You know when you get in to see a specialist the same day of a visit to your primary care physician, something serious is going on, or at least the doctor thinks so. I had asked both my doctor and the cardiologist, "Do you think maybe it is muscular-skeletal?"

Neither of them responded to this suggestion, and neither of them touched my back.

Two cardiologists were in the examination room, one a trainee of some sort. After hearing my answers to questions about family medical history, which included a ridiculous amount of heart disease, one doctor looked at the other and said, "Are you thinking what I'm thinking?" He was. Thus they set me up for an angiogram at eight o'clock the next morning. I went home, called my son, and prepared for a major invasive procedure, which to them was no big deal. To me it was.

I explored the Internet to check out the procedure and discovered women often don't fare well under this scenario, at least not as well as men. Their arteries are smaller and more likely to be punctured. Also, several famous cardiologists endorsed a recent study that reported fifty percent of angiograms are unnecessary. I knew several women who had unfortunate outcomes from them, one of them fatal. What to do?

I decided to trust my intuition; the problem was muscular-skeletal. To test that theory, I dug out The Thumper, a powerful vibrator designed for large body muscles. I acquired it years ago for a back problem. It delivered a pummeling action so severe it made teeth vibrate. The Thumper should never be used anywhere else on the body. A friend visiting me borrowed it one time for her backache and I warned her, "Don't put that on any other place on your body. Seriously."

"Why not?"

"It's for large muscles only. Do not put it on any tender parts. The outcome will not be good."

"How do you know that?"

I lied. "It jarred one of my fillings loose."

The Thumper could pummel you to death if you were in a fragile state, but over the years it had beat tight back muscles into submission. My reaction when I put it on my back this time was similar to a typical response to tasing. The muscles and nerves were so tender I howled and rose from my seat as if I'd been ejected from an airplane cockpit. It was obvious the ache around my shoulder was not a heart problem, and an angiogram was a bad idea.

I cancelled the procedure and insisted on a less invasive test which involved an IV, a scanner, and some sort of nuclear material that could be viewed flowing through arteries. This required I sit with a number of big-bellied, old men in wheelchairs lined up in the heart hospital hallway while being wheeled in and out of treatment rooms throughout the day. At lunchtime, healthcare workers walked by with their Styrofoam containers of food. Bored and hungry, I asked if they were going to eat all that. They were.

The test results revealed no blockage. With this issue resolved, I began a quest for a physical therapist for my shoulder aches. This required I go back to my primary care doctor, who still did not touch my back. At my insistence, she referred me to a physical therapist who called me for an appointment six weeks later. By that time, my back was fine. Daily beatings from The

Thumper, icings, three trips to a massage parlor, and several stress-reducing Comedy Channel marathons, and I was healed.

* * *

Such experiences do not inspire confidence in future healthcare prospects. As I observe friends also being sucked into an array of questionable medical procedures, I am in avoidance mode. This may be a problem someday when a valid treatment is needed, and I'm responding with, "No way."

This doesn't mean I disrespect medical professionals. I don't. They saved three of my grandchildren born with complications, and cardiologists saved my son from the widow-maker heart attack. And they have saved me. God bless them. Still, medical episodes are frustrating and precarious. As a patient, I insist on a high level of involvement so I can tap into the best they have to offer while avoiding the greed-driven downsides of medicine—of drugs in particular.

It is impossible for physicians to keep up-to-date on drug side effects, interactions, and whether risks outweigh benefits. A prescribed drug incapacitated me for months because of tendon, ligament, and muscle damage. Too late, I learned the drug was not appropriate as the first line of treatment for my condition. It's tough to get me to take a drug for anything now. I figure I'd be safer dating a man with a mailbox full of bullet holes.

Friends support my position. One complained a nurse woke him from a deep sleep in the hospital to give him a sleeping pill. A girlfriend complained Viagra turned her husband into a coatrack. And don't get me started on antacid medications or the antibiotic/steroid abyss. Having a good long-term outcome from drugs can be as likely as having the blues in Hawaii.

I'm not anti-medicine, and I admire and appreciate most medical professionals. After imitating a beached whale in my front yard one hot day—the result of heat exhaustion—I took an ambulance ride. Whisked into the typical wait-to-wait emergency room experience, I received hydrating IV's and avoided an all-out heat stroke. Upon release, a doctor warned me I would be more vulnerable to heat stroke in the future and to stay out of the heat that summer.

Avoiding hot environments required lifestyle changes. I cancelled plans to go on an annual event at a lake where friends drank alcoholic beverages and sweated it out all day cruising on a boat. Boating is not a cool-water experience. It does no good to be on the water if you can't get in it.

I had always carpooled to this reunion with two fellows who were determined I go this time in spite of doctor's orders. They were unrelenting. So I came up with another excuse not to go. "I'm pregnant." That did it, but they passed this news on to the folks at the lake and argued all weekend over which one of them was the baby daddy.

* * *

I suspect these unfortunate medical experiences would have been avoided if I still had access to Dr. Willard. Although he was mean to me in the process, he did take care of me.

I walked into his office one day while suffering from a serious case of hives which had caused my neck to blend into my jawline and was about to swell my eyes shut. "What do I do about this?" I asked. Since I had pranked him so many times before, I added, "This is not a joke." That disclosure was not necessary because I looked like the elephant man. After commenting, "It's sad what happened to your face," the good doctor accompanied me to the emergency room where a shot and a prescription were administered. The drug gave me an ulcer that took six months for Dr. Willard to heal.

He accompanied me to the hospital a few months later when there was reason to suspect I had been exposed to anthrax at a Federal facility in Atlanta after 9/11. This happened because I decided to be brave and board one of the first planes to fly after the incident. It was an eery flight. Restless, attentive, large men sat in every aisle seat. I terrorized a young college dance major sitting next to me by suggesting he was an air marshal, which he tolerated good-naturedly. No one stood up during the entire flight. Flight attendants stationed a metal food cart outside the pilot's door. The atmosphere was quiet and tense.

Soon after returning from this trip, the manager of human resources at my company summoned me out of a meeting, marched me into a conference room, and informed me to go to the hospital immediately under an assumed name. I may have been exposed to Anthrax. The blood drained from my face and my stomach tightened into a vice-like grip.

Admitted to the hospital secretly, I was expected to cough up sputum when there wasn't any. Finally, someone said, "I don't think we're going to get any this way." They tried another way. Imagine my relief when Dr. Willard appeared at my bedside and stopped the madness. I was sent home with instructions not to talk to the press. I wasn't much up for talking to the press, although I might have if one of them were a cowboy. (I was in my redneck, macho shithead phase.)

The hospital physician prescribed a powerful drug. I was symptom free, so Dr. Willard, aware of the significant side effects, advised me not to take any pills until the lab results came in from whatever it was they dug out of my throat. He coordinated with the Center for Disease Control and became their point of contact for treating me. He and I were in a meeting when a secretary called him out for a phone call. I fondled a pill in my pocket. When he returned, he gave me a thumbs up, and I knew I didn't have to take it. No one else in the meeting knew what his signal meant except the company president. I knew he knew because he gave me a nod. We never spoke of it.

A few days later, I entered the good doctor's office and asked for Percodan for fat ankles and inquired if there was a pill that would do the same thing as weed. He told me to "Get out!" And he pointed.

Chapter 14

Emergency Room Temptations

Let's Do This Thing

"I love being old," said no one ever. There is nothing soft and mellow about it, but when physical degradation happens, I don't get too upset. I have a mantra: Work the problem. This helped me through a nosebleed crisis necessitating a trip to the emergency room. The setting implied a guaranteed emergency room nightmare except for the potential for glimpses of handsome policemen, firemen, and other men in uniforms who occupy those places late at night.

I drove to the hospital emergency room where I bled on the reception desk and a clipboard of requisite paperwork. After turning it in, the receptionist apparently deemed me not ER worthy. Although I dripped blood on his counter, which he ignored, he instructed me to have a seat in the waiting room.

There I waited, bleeding and scaring small children. Finally, I worked the problem and drove myself home, called an ambulance, and was thereby whisked past the reception desk into the depths of ER hell.

A doctor asked me if I'd had an accident. I said, "No. I picked my nose." He and an intern stifled chuckles and knowingly looked at each other. I said, "Wh-at?" He responded, "You're the first person with a nosebleed to admit to picking your nose. Everyone picks their nose."

I said, "I'm old. I have no dignity left. Why lie?"

He and the intern set to work as my mind pondered:

Have I lost more blood than the pint I would have given if I had donated some? If I ever have sex again, would I have a nosebleed? Would the old fellow?

I didn't share these thoughts since I had enough mental capacity at that point to edit myself. This would soon change.

While the physician set up some intimidating equipment, the intern, who resembled Keith Urban, stood beside my bed, clipboard in hand, asking me medical history questions. I answered while struggling to breathe, swallowing blood, and pinching my nose as per instructions. I responded to his questions about an ingrown toenail, the date of my tonsillectomy in 1968, and when I got my first period.

When Keith Urban asked when I had my last period, I lost my patience, which was never a redeeming quality anyway. I responded, "I'm sixty-seven years old."

Still not getting it, he asked if I was menopausal. I wanted to ask, "What part of sixty-seven do you not understand?" I considered inquiring if he still had his baby teeth, but instead I said again, "I'm sixty-seven years old." A slight smile crossed the lips of the doctor on the other side of the bed. I smiled back, both of us entertained by the innocence of the intern who looked like Keith Urban.

This distraction quickly faded and my eyes pleaded with the doctor. Please help me. The situation was wearing me down. My capacity to filter information waned. I told him and Keith Urban about an old dog named Lucy who was post menopausal and turned into a lesbian.

As I lay there, a handsome uniformed cop in the hall caused me to contemplate my feet. Having left the house in a dither, I wore slippers. Actually, I was a bit of a mess all over— sloppy clothes, bloody hands, chili on my shirt, and hair that resembled a tangle of fishing lures. I mostly wished I'd put on nice shoes, though. My slippers looked like something an old woman would wear, one who was w-a-y past menopause.

For some reason (perhaps it was the resident resembling Keith Urban or the handsome policeman), it occurred to me I no longer knew what I looked like naked. That was undoubtedly a good thing, but it made me feel incredibly old.

On this slippery slope, I worked the problem and forced myself to focus on coping. Nestling into the bed, I introduced breathing exercises and contemplated what color to paint my bedroom. Subtle gray stripes accented with purple accessories and shiny glass objects came to mind. I couldn't wait to get to Home Depot and Z-Gallery.

The doctor instructed me to relax as he stuck a long instrument resembling a cattle prod up my nose. Keith Urban, looking good, observed. I took a deep breath. *Work the problem, Nik, work the problem.*

(Admittedly, this serious essay does not match the tone or topic of this book. Propaganda is not even near sexy, except perhaps to greedy manipulators inside and outside of this country. However, this may be my last book, and I must have my say. The message is crucial given the nature of propaganda today and how people are embracing it.)

Chapter 15

Reflections on the Void of Cognizance

*Learn as though you will live forever. . .*Gandhi

Those who stop seeking live in a shallow haze. Poet Dylan Thomas described this condition: "Someone is boring me. I think it's me." Melancholy is incompatible with learning. Joyful people move beyond ignorance into the glow of enlightenment. They never give in to the feeling of knowing enough.

When people are marginalized, the absence of learning is the culprit. Simplistic views and conspiracy theories are accepted without question. Through ignorance, these folks are susceptible to exploitation by self-serving, unscrupulous shysters who use biased rhetoric, online madness, raging media commentators, and the dangerous phenomenon of groupthink to manipulate. These divisive influences have polarized our society to the point of malfunction.

———————————————————

To search for the truth
in a fact-adverse culture,
seek news versus spin.

To be an astute, learned individual, a person must keep up with what is happening in the world. This is a tricky undertaking because much of today's news is not news. It is commentary embellished with misrepresented facts designed to manipulate. This nonsense information is so ridiculous it is as though a body sat up in a coffin. Still, many people have abandoned critical thinking, which has created a national malaise of believing whatever preposterous information is dished out.

The proliferation of talk radio, the Internet, and twenty-four-hour news sources desperate to fill schedules are the underbelly of news today. Many older people—brought up in an era when news was real and the agenda of those delivering it was truth and objectivity—don't realize that both the source and the content of news today are suspect.

Much of today's news is outright propaganda sold as fact and designed to influence people to act against their own best interests. Opportunists finance distorted news intended to misinform, control, and exploit. The goal is to convince people they are disenfranchised victims and to define their views for them. Once done, those people are used for the manipulators' purposes. The motivation is power and greed.

These master manipulators harvest souls, preach the gospel of fear, and lead susceptible victims like terrified sheep over a metaphorical cliff of hate. They distract from political issues by introducing moral ones outside the scope of government. News is bad enough without these distortions. A person must choose whether to take it in or to remain sane.

Manipulators use fear to influence. Older people tend to view the world through the filtered lens of apprehension. So susceptibility to exploitation through fear increases with age. Many are unwittingly influenced by biased news sources and negative commentary rich with subversive bigotry cleverly designed to induce fear, convince them they are victims, and fuel their anger.

Every source of news has an agenda. For some, it is to objectively gather and share information. For others, it's to distort news for their own purposes. Greedy, charismatic commentators with inflated senses of self-importance get rich by inducing people to not think. A person can acknowledge this reality or choose to internalize whatever rubbish these creeps serve up.

Belongingness thrives
when someone else thinks for you,
but you are wasted.

Media manipulators capitalize on the powerful human dynamic of groupthink. They isolate by convincing their audiences that all other sources of information are unreliable. Once all information is funneled through the manipulators' filters, an alternative reality is fostered, one that magnifies fears. Through that source, enemies are manufactured so victims bind together against a common foe. Postured to release the mother load of crazy, exploiters knit tormented souls together so tightly there is no margin for individual thought.

It is difficult for people who don't think like the manipulators to realize the degree to which these schemers embrace a self-serving mentality. Audiences are like the jury unable to visualize a Manson-type mad man as a murderer when the guy is cleaned up and dressed for court. They don't see the picture taken when he was arrested with his filthy, unshaven face, tattered clothes, matted hair, bare feet, and blank, evil eyes.

A basic tribal need causes people to seek leaders and to rally around them—to follow. This is good when the leader is altruistic and has the well-being of the masses at heart. But, when loyalty is surrendered to profiteering, manipulative, self-serving leaders, and the beliefs they espouse are blindly accepted no matter how illogical or damaging they are to followers, it is not good. Groupthink prevails and rational judgment, critical thinking, and logical interpretations are abandoned. In this scenario, otherwise reasonable people embrace the outrageous. History is flush with examples of groupthink gone bad. Our country is rife with folks immersed in it.

Under this scenario, associations, alliances, and religions are used to persuade people to support the very corporate establishment and government corruption that is crushing them. Self-serving seekers of power, money, or attention build fortunes on the misfortunes of others and play those blindly supporting them like fine guitars.

_____

When one tests the truth
and exposes illusions,
beliefs become soft.

Groupthink creates right fighters—people who believe they are blessed with all the answers and who try to force them on others. With no awareness that the thoughts in their heads are impressions in the mind, not facts, right fighters are incapable of evaluating information. Highly judgmental of those with differing opinions, they become enraged, arrogant bullies.

Inflamed by manipulative media sources fueling the fires of discontent, these right fighters become hell bent on insisting others accept their beliefs—an impossible prospect. The failure to convert others causes them to feel even more victimized. In turn, they become raging persecutors. When their victims fight back, a vicious cycle of persecution and victimization is manifested.

Dr. Phil McGraw asks, "Do you want to be right, or do you want to be happy?" Groupthink leaders are vested in perpetuating the discontented, enraged victim roles of their constituency. This requires that right-fighting followers be unhappy, hold to their beliefs tightly, and ignore information that doesn't support those beliefs. The relentless pressure for such followers to act against their own best interests is so formidable that they are like turkeys voting for Thanksgiving.

The propensity of individuals to accept the illogical and ridiculous should not be underestimated. Otherwise intelligent and cogent people will believe anything if it provides a fix for "their ruin." Manipulators—who know groupthink is a powerful phenomenon deeply engrained in the human psyche—exploit the power tapping into ruin offers.

Lies teamed up with facts
should nibble at your conscience,
else you are a fool.

Here is how shrewd media pontificators use groupthink to manipulate: They take a nugget of truth and build distorted, fear-based information around it. Because there is that nugget of truth in there somewhere, people accept all the information as true, when much of it is not. Negative catch-phrases and key words become verbal calories repeated over and over to sell the exploiter's position. They pound away until their points are knitted into the bones of their listeners. Joseph Goebbels, Adolf Hitler's propaganda minister, said, "If you repeat a lie often enough, it becomes the truth." Some of these beliefs are so bizarre that to a rational person it's like someone is playing "I Left My Heart in San Francisco" on the piano while a singer sings "My Way." Something is off.

People are receptive to information that supports what they already believe, so manipulators frame messages around popular core beliefs. When people become convinced someone supports their core beliefs, those beliefs are used to introduce enemies and fear. When done again and again, fear becomes addictive—a drug that induces rage. People give up their ability to think for themselves. This is a brilliant, subversive strategy. Once people rage as a group, it's hard to turn the frenzy around. No amount of logic will do it. The winners in this scenario are manipulators. Everyone else loses.

Boldness and courage
cause a rational thinker
to seek evidence.

What can a person do to avoid falling prey to manipulators in a non-evidence-based society? Ask this question when evaluating sources of information: *Does someone make money, gain power, or get attention and adoration by persuading me to embrace their convictions?*

When the fortresses of greed claim "no spin," look for the spin. When a source of information claims everyone else is biased, look for their bias. (Objective news sources don't brag about objectivity. It goes without saying.) Hold beliefs lightly. Be open to fresh information. Change your mind when new information surfaces. Base opinions on facts, solid sources, and logical analysis instead of groundless dogma.

Wise people land on both sides of the political spectrum because their opinions are derived issue by issue rather than from political loyalties and from what they are told to think. Considering situations issue by issue is the measure of an astute, independent thinker who refuses to be a pawn.

————————————————

When you say nothing,
when you don't challenge nonsense,
you're endorsing it.

Be the voice of reason. Challenge misrepresented facts. You don't have to argue. Respond to ridiculous statements with this: "I'm sorry if the facts don't line up with your narrative," or "I believe you believe that, but I don't." Or ask: "Just because you think something in your head, does that make it true?" If an ardent right fighter insists irrational thoughts are real, one lady makes a point by saying: "Wow! This means if I think unicorns exist, they do. I'm so excited."

A brave, enlightened person is not influenced by greedy, wealthy people controlling the media, people who sit around on their yachts *not* wondering what the poor people are doing. He speaks out against misinformation. When someone advocates malarkey, silence is interpreted by that person, and anyone else present, as agreement. Silence does not have a neutral influence. It is endorsement.

——————————————

*You can influence
and create a legacy
that shines forever.*

If you are frustrated and confused by this, you are not alone. Many people fall prey to expert manipulators. A misinformed person cannot be an effective, respected leader of a family. Wouldn't you rather be a wise, insightful old sage than an old fool? You can be. By seeking enlightenment and challenging the unreasonable, you demonstrate rational-thinking and avoid appearing foolish to friends, children, and grandchildren. Don't underestimate your ability to analyze facts and evidence, interpret them, apply logic and rational thought, and draw your own conclusions. If you abdicate these functions to others, you could end up riding a fanciful unicorn, or worse.

Neutered

The truth is dead
The Internet killed it.

The news is biased
Politics abused it.

The public got screwed
And never knew it.

(In memory of Mom, a consummate worrier, this award-winning potpourri of meanderings is a compilation of incidents from my memoir, *Red Heels and Smokin'* and other pieces I've written.)

Chapter 16

The Worry Gene

*At age twenty we worry about what others think of us. At age forty, we don't care what they think of us. At age sixty, we discover they haven't been thinking of us at all. . .*Ann Landers

My life is a mosaic of worries. An equal opportunity worrier, I worry about everything. I worry I'll end up at an ATM in a casino, Miley will outsell Beyonce, and I'll be injured by a rock under a Slip N Slide. I worry I'll have sheet marks on my face on a breakfast date and airport security will discover a device vibrating in my carry-on luggage. I fret over any good fortune because it is surely the universe playing a trick, and it won't last.

Being an expert worrier—an aficionado of sorts—doesn't mean I respond properly to the incidents I worry about. When tornado sirens go off, rather than take shelter, I go outside to look for one. I do worry, though—that a piece of flying sheet metal will cut off my head, a cow will land on me, or a near-miss, airborne BMW will break my glasses.

I began worrying about near-sex experiences in my sixties. When I was younger, I had real sex experiences to worry about. Now, things are different. My worries center on such things as the man in my retiree coffee group who announced his carburetor leaked and he wasn't talking about his car. Then there was the old fellow who encountered a dessert topped with powdered sugar and put some in his nose. I shouldn't worry about men, though. Landing one at my age is a long shot. As one friend said, "I never meet a man I'd take my teeth out for." I have a full set of teeth —well, almost—and I worry whether that is an asset or a liability. And I worry about keeping them.

My worrisome nature was acquired honestly. Mom, an Iowa farm woman, inherited the worry gene and passed it down. When I took her on a trip to Salt Lake City, she worried the mountains around the city would slide in on us. When I called us *Thelma and Louise* on road trips, she was afraid she would be the one who shot somebody. When I began cavorting with Democrats, she worried I would turn into a socialist, communist and join a union. When I moved to Oklahoma, she fretted about me taking up with an Indian (which I did). When my daughter moved to California, Mom worried she would marry a foreigner (which she did). On a trip to Hawaii, Mom complained, "This place is full of foreigners."

Concerns about foreigners created anxiety over a trip to Mexico. So I decided to learn some Spanish. A friend taught me what he claimed was a welcoming phrase that actually translated to, "Don't fuck with me, buddy." I realized it was not a welcoming phrase when my driver and a hotel clerk didn't take to it. I also learned that "quesadillas" does not mean "to have a good day." When I wished a taxi driver a good day, he dropped me off at a food cart.

I worry about tennis balls. Plastic surgeons can tell which side a person sleeps on just by looking at their face. They recommend people sleep on their backs. Tennis balls sewn on the front of pajamas prevent a person from rolling over onto their stomach in the night. I worry that the unfortunate placement of balls could create a near-sex experience. Or, if I died in my sleep and my family discovered tennis balls sewn onto the front of my pajamas, my grandson would say, "I told you Grandma was c-a-a-r-r-a-z-y." So I'm stuck with a face that looks like an unfortunate crochet project.

I worry about boyfriends. I thought a quiet, mellow fellow was mysterious. Turns out, he was just stupid. I had to talk him out of going discount bungie jumping. He had quite an appetite, so I worried he would eat my potpourri. He wouldn't use a seat belt because he wanted to be "thrown clear," which was worrisome because he drove a car like he stole it. And he was a master of disorganization. To him the plan was always that there was no plan. The man was a go-getter, though. He'd take me to work and then go get me.

I was not a priority in his life. He refused to do anything about his turkey, Trombone, who attacked me when I got out of my car. His dog, Milton, sat on my face when I did yoga. I ended the relationship when I realized the glitter in his eyebrows was from a stripper—not a craft project. Since he often went to the liquor store for breakfast, he was drunk when I broke up with him, so I had to do it again the next day. He didn't take it well, and I worried he would post a message on bathroom walls suggesting men call me for a mediocre time.

To help me over the breakup, friends took me clubbing. It was there I met Leroy, a fellow who embraced the profession of waiting for his next court appearance. He flattered me by saying I was prettier than a John Deere Tractor. Leroy stuck to me like a tree frog. He only had one upper front tooth, which reminded me of a can opener. He might have come in handy if I went camping, but I don't go camping.

A burly man intervened and ran Leroy off by belly-bumping him and asking, "What part of 'no' do you not understand?" Soon I had to worry about this man who said, "You sure do have nice child bearin' hips."

I advised my friends not to take me to any more clubs that look like prison waiting rooms where I have to worry about a whacked-out, surly man in need of a drug test and on the verge of turning into a pet rock loafing on my sofa. That night I dreamed about the ugliest man in Fairmont County who took me on a date to a cock fight after which I washed his truck and stocked his trailer with a fly swatter.

Being single and being thrust into the dating scene exaggerated my tendency to worry. I became concerned about drinking too much and saying to someone like Leroy, "Am I sexy yet?" I worried about dating younger men and having jalapeño poppers at Sonic on a dinner date followed by great sex on a futon. If I dated older ones, I might wake up in the morning in an AARP t-shirt. Then there was the guy who, on the third date, said he loved me more than beer, which I did not believe because of the breathalyzer in his beat up Ram diesel 4x4 truck.

I dabbled in Internet dating. Since I didn't embrace astrological tenets, I listed my astrological sign as Feces. This attempt at comedic expression soon generated concern that online prospects did not *get* my sense of humor. Asparagus would have been a better choice.

The problem with Internet dating is that people who lie on the Internet complain that people lie on the Internet, myself included. I checked the box on my profile that indicated I was *fit, toned, and athletic* when I was *soft, fluffy, and Rubenesque,* and not necessarily in that order. Worse yet, I had photoshopped my picture. This process yielded some fabulous virtual plastic surgery, but it also generated grave concerns. Men would expect the woman in the photo, and I would show up.

There were other Internet dating worries. After learning my profession was teaching, a man asked if I would spank him. A fellow who claimed to be ambulatory was obviously not going to be ambulatory long. Fergus was so Irish I wanted him to go be Irish someplace else. Mullet boasted about financial security and then bragged he didn't pay taxes— ever. Herb had a masters in fine arts and lived with his parents. I avoided men with names of animals or verbs, and only an idiot would date a man with the call name Gameboy. I may be a mess, but I moved past the frat boy stage fifty-some years ago.

The Internet madness ended when I took up with Hank. At that point, I had to worry about my girlfriends discovering that Hank and I celebrated my birthday at a Bass Pro Shop and that my gift was a leaf blower. For Christmas, I got a steer-horn belt buckle and homemade deer jerky. I told the girls, "Hank's a sweetie. He gave me jewelry, and he cooked for me."

Hank is of the redneck breed. These men have a soft spot for women who mow, and they jack up their trucks because fat girls can't climb. So I fret about grass growing and gaining weight. Not only that, Hank was clean-shaven when we met. Now an overachieving beard has taken over, and he has abandoned haircuts. I worry I married a Chia Pet.

Rednecks believe *Die Hard* is a Christmas movie, and they have a fondness for surround sound. Hank stood behind me at the checkout counter in a book store with his book on wiring for surround sound. I was purchasing a couple of crime books about black widow women who killed their husbands. The curious clerk asked Hank if my book selections made him nervous. He responded, "It hadn't, but now that you mention it. . . ." In my mind, his book was the real threat. Surround sound had the potential to ruin my life. I used to think surround sound was a rich people problem, but no-o-o-o. Every poor boy has surround sound, even if he sleeps on a mattress on the floor, drinks coffee out of a red Solo cup, and has no toilet paper in his trailer.

* * *

When I'm not worrying about Hank, I'm concerned about friends. Cookie, who spent what was probably too many years in the Army, is capable of getting into a girl fight. Pepper, fresh out of prison for embezzlement, has a job at a payday loan company. Evie is depressed over excessive weight gain. Hank and I took her to a party to cheer her up. When a man there made a remark to Hank about rolling Evie in flour and targeting the wet spots, I had to worry whether the blood would wash out of his pearl-snap western shirt.

Cookie asked me to stand up with her at her wedding at a biker rally. This caused me to worry I might be expected to show my titties there. She arranged for security from some fellow named Dirty. When I asked her if I could call him Dirt for short, she said that might ruin the wedding—and possibly the rally.

I worried about her biker friends. There were strong indications some of these folks were not taking their medication. Brute had an unconcealed weapon velcro-ed to his leg and a t-shirt that said, "I don't call 911." Grunt, a biker with an ankle monitor, offered me a ride to the southern point of South America on his Harley. Fortunately, Hank stayed home the day of the wedding to watch Olympic curling, so I didn't have to concern myself with his face being rearranged while defending my honor. Nevertheless, I worried whether or not he would have done so had he been there.

Even my hairdresser, Lilly, introduces worries. Her over-processed hair resembles sofa stuffing, and it is a different primary color with each appointment. I worry she'll turn my hair into something resembling a cat toy. Her boyfriend has several misspelled tattoos, vampire teeth, and a row of piercings down each ear. I could go on, but you get the picture. So I worry where Lilly is headed. Jail, probably, when a cop car lights him up and he slips drugs into her purse. He'll get a new girlfriend and never visit Lilly in jail.

The digital age introduces grave concerns. If the tape over the camera on my laptop falls off, someone might see me loading the dishwasher naked. The online test to discover the color of a person's aura might determine mine is plaid, or houndstooth, or, worse yet, ecru. It is wise to worry over technical issues. I know what the geeks who rescue me are thinking: *I'm from tech support, and I'm here to make you feel stupid.*

Outdoor activities are intimidating. I worry about sticks, rocks, dirt, bugs, spiders, ticks, snakes, mold, pollen, and weather in general. If my dead body is found at a campsite, I worry whether investigators will figure out I was murdered someplace else and dumped there because I don't go outdoors.

My friend, Baxter, is a concern because he believes marijuana is a condiment. He sits at stop signs waiting for them to turn green. Baxter persuaded me to try a toke, which made my teeth feel big. I ate a whole box of Fruit Loops and the best carrots in the universe. "Baxter, where did you get these awesome carrots?"

"They're talented musical carrots, dude."

"I'm not a dude." Should I worry I've not looked at carrots the same since or that Baxter called me a dude?

I worry my therapist will abandon my treatment plan and prescribe drugs instead. Perhaps it was a bad idea to tell him about my nude hang-gliding fantasy, that I named my vibrator Sam Elliot, or the appeal of men who are like dumpster fires.

Prescription drugs are scary. In addition to worrisome side effects, pills are often a different shape and color with every refill. I worry they are male hormones and I'll grow a mustache.

Aging promotes foreboding and unrelenting worries about deteriorating mental capacity. When I lost my reading glasses *and* the backup pair, I found both in the shower—one on my face and the other on my head. So I acquired a memory-enhancing herb. But because I don't want to remember everything, I only take half doses. I don't want to remember Wally.

My posture is a concern. I worry I'll become so stooped I'll turn into one of those people who, when seen from behind, appears to not have a head.

Even food sparks concerns. Who can resist a cinnamon roll the size of a small dog? Since bacon is a protein and ice cream a source of calcium, my arms have taken on the appearance of legs, my stomach sticks out so far security officers at the airport pat it down, and from the side I look like Africa.

Today, I worry there are Zombies living in my attic who got their freak on last night and snuck down to hide the remote and eat my last PayDay candy bar.

Are they starving up there? Will they eat the insulation? Will an ear fall off and attract rodents?

Chapter 17

And Then, There Was Roger

Uncouth Squared

There is something not right about Roger. A sort of quintessential renegade, he is irreverent to the nth degree and not the kind of guy you want to put on the speaker phone if your mother is present.

As the greeter at a Christmas party, his welcome message was "Merry fucking Christmas and Happy goddamn New Year." The only things preventing Roger from having his face rearranged were the deplorable nature of the venue, which discouraged high expectations; Roger's festive holiday elf costume; and an endearing, disarming smile that unfurled across his face like syrup on a pancake. No one was more fun than my friend Roger.

Mother and I were sitting at my kitchen table when Roger called. She had never met him. I answered with the speaker phone on, and a voice, loud and clear, said, "You wanna fuck?"

I was horrified and amused at the same time. The look on Mom's face said it all. Her mind bounced frantically between shock and dismay. A right and proper Iowa farm woman with a WASP (white, Anglo-Saxon, Protestant) mentality, she was perplexed by my urban lifestyle. This caused her to worry about the dangers I surely faced on a regular basis as a single woman in the mad city of Tulsa, Oklahoma. Wispy disco dresses and four-inch platform heels in my closet did nothing to dispel those fears. Now she would worry about Roger.

"Roger, my mother is sitting here. She can hear you."

"Does she wanna fuck?"

As that suggestion stormed into her, Mom's eyes widened, her mouth dropped, blood drained from her face, and she squirmed in her chair. As she regrouped, her expression took on the *Saturday Night Live* Church Lady persona that evangelistic women show when appalled. Over the years, I had seen this look many times, but this time the image took on a particularly vivid presentation.

I was in a similar panic. The phone felt like a mass of hot coals. As Roger moved on to the coming weekend's party report, which implied we partied like coked-up rock stars, his uncouth proposition continued to simmer in Mom's head. No doubt, she had never before had such an offer.

Roger's normal response to being judged was to rebel and frolic briskly between obnoxiousness and offensiveness. In rare form, he bounced intentionally between tidbits designed to gross out my mother. "The Bouncin' Boobies Club acquired a new strobe light. Charlie Sheen describes his penis as a heat-seeking missile. And Keith Richards has an impressive dildo collection."

"Roger, let's contemplate something more relevant."

"Oh, sure. Did you know if you masturbate with your left hand, it feels like it's someone else doing it?"

"Oh, my god, that does it. You're done." I looked over and was surprised to see a big smile on Mom's face. Her eyes twinkled, and her body bounced as she giggled. She realized no one would be that offensive unintentionally, and, no doubt, she found humor in my discomfort. I loved the way her eyes sparkled when she giggled.

She leaned over and whispered, "Tell Roger I'm already spoken for."

When I finally got rid of him, she suggested, "There is something wrong with Roger."

"Yes, I know. But he has a good heart."

A Candidate for Social Reconstruction

Before you were born, your plight was set.
You were a boy and all that meant.
You blasted and blundered with no regret.
And seduced every one of the women you met.

Sometimes uncouth, sometimes misguided,
You sweet-talked girls, but love was one-sided.
Like a coyote in a pack of poodles,
You chased and shook and left them in puddles.

As though a camera zooming in,
You picked prey, determined to win.
But you couldn't give away what you didn't have.
So excuses and apologies became the salve.

A problem's not solved with the mind that made it,
You required social reconstruction, but you hated it.
Then a woman arrived who considered you fine.
She polished you up and delivered the shine.

Now a minivan makes your testicles shrink.
But you can't ignore a little girl's wink.
Face it, man, you had a good whirl,
But ultimately you got beat by a girl.

Chapter 18

Infatuation

Dog Hair and Disco Sequins

Calvin, a Dalmatian, wanted me—bad. He was my daughter, Mel's, dog. She and her boyfriend acquired him as a puppy when they were students at college, thereby demonstrating the lack of good judgement common among young people who couple up and respond to the nesting instinct by acquiring a pet they can neither afford nor take care of. But it was done, and there was Calvin on campus at Oklahoma State University.

Someone told me Dalmatians aren't known for being the most intelligent breed. I don't know if that's true, but Calvin seemed to fit that mold. He made up for it with his lovable, devoted temperament, and he found his niche among freshman students in a small rent house just off campus.

When I visited there, Calvin followed me everywhere, stared at me longingly, tried to get in my lap, and occasionally hunched my leg. I lay in bed one morning awake but eyes still closed when the feeling of another presence in the room overtook me. I opened one eye to discover Calvin resting his chin on the bed an inch or two from my face, staring intently. We engage in a mutual stare-down until I threw the covers off, which thrust him into a state of excitement only a dog can experience. His toenails clicked loudly on the floor as he turned in circles and hopped around like a wind-up toy.

I called for my daughter to corral him long enough for a respite in the bathroom after which he followed me around the rest of the day. And so there we were, Calvin in love, me not so much, and my daughter in the middle.

As so often is the case, she and her boyfriend broke up. He got custody of Calvin in spite of the dog's intense attachment to Mel. Years later, the ex-boyfriend found Mel on the Internet and asked if she would take Calvin for six weeks while he took an out-of-town training program for his job. She agreed.

They arranged to meet on a California beach to make the transfer. Mel stood near the water as her ex and Calvin moseyed down the beach toward her—Calvin unaware of what was to transpire. He bounded around on the beach, running in and out of the water as dogs do. Suddenly he stopped and sniffed the air. He stood rigid, staring into the distance. Mel stood there not moving. Suddenly, he bounded in her direction, kicking up sand as he sprinted like a Greyhound. The heartwarming reunion was reminiscent of videos of veterans returning home to dogs whose enthusiasm could knock out a tooth or put out an eye.

Mel had no intention of telling me about her babysitting assignment. I never thought getting a dog was a good idea for poor, underfunded college students and discouraged her from keeping him when the kids broke up. No doubt, I would have not thought the babysitting arrangement a good idea either since Mel worked long hours. (Turns out, Calvin became a popular character at the office—a mascot of sorts.) With my narrow, closely held opinions, it's easy to understand why she withheld the news of Calvin's stay from me. I figured it out, though. Months after Calvin's visit ended, I visited my daughter. Calvin hairs turned up on my black clothes. It had taken years for me to divest my wardrobe of Calvin hairs and disco sequins. Now the hairs were back—a clue something was up.

Mel fessed up. She described the touching reunion on the beach. Sweet Calvin got one more dose of Mel, her boyfriend went off to training with his dog in good hands, and I resurrected memories of a canine who probably wanted me more than any man ever did.

Joey

She spotted him under the table, excited and nervous,
  his little tail slicing the air like windshield wipers.

A baby, barely weaned, he was companionless,
  alone with an owner who was rarely home.

She dropped to the floor and crawled under the table,
  uttering sweet, high-pitched, little girl babytalk.

They bonded through giggles and squeaky puppy barks.
  There was no going back. He was hers, and she was his.

Driving home, I glanced back into the back seat.
  Sitting upright in her lap, he looked square at me.

His eyes spoke more than words ever could.
  "I am in my place."

Chapter 19

French Cafe Slouch

*The Juju of Fuck-Me Shoes,
and the Panache of Pantsuits.*

At three a.m., in a New York City all-night cafe, I
observed rumpled, tipsy, scantily dressed young women
parading by in wobbly four-inch heels. Testosterone-
fueled young men in the next booth delivered a pickup
line: "Oh my god! You are so beautiful. Oh my god!" One
gal's mini dress had hiked up so high the crotch of her
thong was visible in the front and her bare ass in the
back. The guys were so taken by *thong girl* that they
pounded the table. Unable to contain themselves, they
rose from their seats as if their butts were filled with
helium. Omitting the "You are so beautiful," they just
said, "Oh, my god! Oh, my god! Oh, my god!" as they
followed her down the aisle. (*Red Heels and Smokin'*)

Those boys didn't notice me, of course. As a writer, I
dressed like a French cafe slouch and was still trying to lose
baby fat from my firstborn child forty-eight years ago.

During the years I worked, though, I embraced style, which was not entirely a vanity proposition. I aspired to be a professional woman and believed appearance was important for a woman in the business world. Black pantsuits paired with red high heels never failed to inspire self-confidence, and the power suits of those career days gave me moxie. How I dress now as a writer has its own juju, but it's a far cry from that sophisticated image I once exhibited with pride.

In the 1970's, if a woman wanted to climb the corporate ladder, a severe, conservative style mandated by men and society was required. The book *Dress for Success* set the rules by proposing a "uniform" approach for women—a look reminiscent of men's suits, only with a feminine touch. This included a dark skirt and jacket; a pastel, oxford, buttoned-down-collared blouse similar to a man's shirt; and a scarf tied at the neck somewhat representative of a man's tie. Hose were required. Sensible pumps completed the look. This look resembled the uniform of an airline stewardess. With an accompanying rolling travel bag and a trendy page boy hairdo, employees at airports and hotels, who were unaccustomed to women's business dress, assumed I was a flight attendant and offered me airline employee discounts.

In the late 1970's, women successfully lobbied against the ban on pantsuits and won. This was a major breakthrough. I recall the outrageously trendy feeling I experienced the first time I wore a pantsuit to work. In the mode of Amelia Earhart and Katharine Hepburn, a sense of panache—of being free and more powerful—pervaded. This gave me a taste of how men must feel not being restrained by skirts, girdles, hose, and ridiculously uncomfortable shoes.

About this time, disco became popular and platform heels became a fashion statement. Heels with straps around the ankles, known as "fuck-me" shoes, were also trending. I wore such contraptions to work and danced in them at night. Even today, there is nothing sexier than "fuck-me" shoes, except perhaps cleavage. Cleavage at the office trumps everything else if a woman is foolish enough to blatantly display her globes of pleasure in a den full of power-mongering *Mad Men*.

In the 1980's, professional dress leaned toward dark, conservative business suits accented with colorful blouses. This changed for me when Margaret Thatcher spoke at a seminar while wearing a bright, shiny, royal blue silk suit. Sitting in the back row of the theater, I couldn't tell if Margaret wore "fuck-me" shoes, but I bet not. Her shoes were most likely something similar to what the Queen would wear. In spite of insipid shoes, the strong color of her suit was impressive. It implied power—woman power. With that influence, I added vivid-colored suits to my wardrobe.

Wearing color was something dashing women could do that men could not. Finally, we had an edge. While men endeavored to look large in meetings by spreading their bodies out like peacocks spread their tails and propping up their chairs, I sat unassumingly in my royal blue or garnet red suit knowing I was, by god, somebody.

Observing Sigourney Weaver authoritatively bossing people around in the movie *Working Girl*, I gravitated to high-fashion suits, pearls, and chic heels. Sophistication became key. During this phase, I watched Hillary Clinton as First Lady at a State of the Union Address in a suit I had hanging in my closet. I knew then I had found the right professional style.

During this time, serious professional women were power dressing while many painfully ignorant young girls at the office demonstrated no sense of the notion of different dress for different settings. They overdressed or underdressed. Blatantly unaware of the consequences of appearance, or unabashedly not caring about making an impression, rules of propriety were ignored. Even sharp, confident, career-oriented young women exhibited the flair of drum majorettes, and some dressed like wannabe cheerleaders, ice skaters, or go-go dancers.

Skimpy sundresses made me want to ask. "Where's the picnic?" Slinky, shiny dresses suggested a disco dance would break out at any moment. Girls advertising the flowering of their fertility dressed like hoochie mommas leaning into windows of pickup trucks on Eleventh Street. As our culture cured, girls blatantly bared midriffs, revealing pierced bellybuttons, roses and hearts peaking out above belt-lines, and lightning bolt tattoos shooting out of butt cracks. When these girls bent over to get into file drawers, strings of thongs drove the poor men c-a-r-r-a-a-zy. In a state of constant fear of sexual harassment charges, they straightened ties and jiggled change in their pockets.

On the other end of the spectrum were those, young and old, who came to work looking as though they were off to a tractor pull, a cock fight, or a float trip. Some wore sagging t-shirt fabric on tops and bottoms, which gave off a pajama or a POW vibe. Then there were those to whom you could toss a rifle and they were ready to hunt. A few appeared to be farmers headed out to put up hay. I couldn't help but wonder, *What part of "business casual" do you folks not understand?*

Today, these looks are accepted attire, especially in business settings where millennials settle into bean bags to do their jobs. The rigid formalities of the *Mad Men* era are gone. I miss the fancy dress occasionally, but mostly, as a retired person and a writer, I'm giving in to the comfort factor. I still cover up body parts. If I'm wearing a thong, no one is going to know it. I rarely wear heels, make-up seldom happens, and I've never been one to want to reveal cleavage, especially at the office. I leave being the boob fairy to others.

Today, I don't aspire to look like a sassy, hot momma or a well-dressed fashion maven. I don't want to work that hard. I prefer to look like I feel—like a soft, well-worn flannel shirt that brushes the skin lightly, soothes the soul, and cradles the spirit. And I'm okay if I have a tragic hair-do, mismatched earrings, and arms the size of Jabba the Hutt's. Vanity is an internal thing, and there is freedom in acknowledging that no one cares what I look like but me. My look may be unimaginative, but my actions, well, that's another thing. Sometimes I do things I shouldn't.

The Absence of Prudence

I aspire to an appropriate level of dignity,
but nice is boring and the refined tedious.

So I do things I shouldn't—irreverent, inappropriate,
gonzo-crazy things.

Like a third-base coach waving a runner home,
I encourage others to do the same.

My child hears of these escapades and threatens,
"Don't make me come over there."

Chapter 20

A Place to Write

Every woman needs a room of her own. . . . Virginia Wolf

Panera Bread Company is my happy place, my *Cheers,* a place where everyone knows my name. When I'm in publishing mode, I must work at home to have access to files. When I'm in writing mode, or coaching a writer, or judging a contest, I'm at *my office,* Panera Bread Company.

I usually arrive at six in the morning when it opens. Like in the *Cheers* sitcom, regular Panera customers sit in the same spots every day and commune with workers and each other. Occasionally, innocent interlopers arrive ahead of the regulars and sit in their spots. As regulars filter in and surround that person, they move on. No one is rude. Good manners prevail, but being surrounded by chatty people who all know each other is a powerful defender of territory.

Jackie is our Sam Malone. She fills orders and calls regulars by name, or by a colorful nickname. A well-dressed, sophisticated fellow has the incongruent label of *Knot-head* because he showed up one day with a bump on his forehead from a fall. Jackie was not going to pass that up. She hasn't given me a nickname yet. Perhaps I'm not that interesting. She calls my friend Phoebe because she looks like a character on *Friends,* which makes me think she should call me Rachel because I look like Jennifer Aniston.

I always get a good parking place in front of the building because I'm the first one there. When Jackie sees me pull up, she gets my order started. Panera has been robbed twice in the early morning hours. Both times were on rare days I didn't go there. So now, when I pull up in front at 6:00, I sit in my car in the dark and peer in to make sure Jackie is puttering around inside and not huddled in the back room with a gun to her head. If I don't see her or anyone else, I sit in the car until I do.

Regular customers come into Panera in waves. The six o'clock group includes a few other people and myself. We are serious, early morning dolts. Little socialization occurs, except with Jackie who greets each one of us with some sort of banter.

That changes when the 7:00 customers totter in. At this point, I'm surrounded by a bunch of Republicans. Several old, retired fellows settle in on my right and a few working conservatives cluster to my left. We sit in the same spots every day in a line of tables along a wall. Fans of the gospel of the Tea

Party and Fox News, they stew around in victim mode, blaming Obama for the weather, the low job rate (which is actually high), and a war started by a Republican. They are like dogs barking at cars. Improvement in the national debt, the salvation of the auto industry, stock market record highs, and a slew of other positive financial indicators are ignored. They manage to find some piece of information to gripe about. I say to them, "Is that all you got?" Occasionally, I'll ask how their IRAs are doing just to remind them something they care about is unarguably better. When I do so, their eyes glaze over, and they pivot. They cannot deal with anything being good about this President.

We've achieved a peaceful coexistence. One day as the hateful talk proliferated beyond a level of tolerance for me, I shut my laptop and picked up my purse to leave. They insisted I stay and moderated their dialogue. They've done so ever since, which I find remarkable because they hate so hard. But I appreciate their accommodation.

In spite of our political differences, we developed enough mutual respect to find comfort in camaraderie. Then the 2016 election happened, and hate escalated. Vehement discussions with fanatical, illogical, nonsensical opinions grated on me. I've never been one to define myself by what I am anti about, but this was too much. I could no longer tolerate the ridiculous, offensive remarks. Though not an elegant solution, I relocated to the other side of the room when I realized I could no longer temper my responses. Sad. Bigly sad. But I took the advice I often gave my children: Not all friendships are forever and it's okay to let go when they become toxic or simply no longer feed the spirit.

Around eight-thirty, a large group of boisterous Democrats gather. The Republicans consider them radical socialist, vegan, atheist, lesbian communists who work for The Department of Redundancy and hold the outrageous opinion all citizens should be able to vote and have access to healthcare. One of these radicals is known as The Mayor of Panera because he makes rounds every day to make certain everyone feels welcome.

Around nine o'clock, my Panera boyfriend arrives. He's a legal expert and a motorcycle dude some fifteen years my junior. In the landscape of men, he is an appealing fellow who tells me if I would just give him the word, he'd drop his girlfriend for me. His level of insincerity is astounding. I've seen pictures of his girlfriend, who is beautiful and significantly more age appropriate. He shines and sparkles when he talks about her.

The man pretends to be smitten, but he is the epitome of a rascal and gets no traction with me. The burden of experience has taught me younger men are hard to hold. Although the thought of romance occasionally does a fanciful dance in my imagination, the prospect of my actually having a relationship with any man has been tucked so far into the recesses of my mind a Dyson couldn't suck it out. I suspect this emboldens him. I'm safe.

I like to think the appeal is my sparkling personality and charm but more likely it is the phenomenon that as you get really old, you become cute again. Not young cute, but geriatric cute. By the time I'm ninety, I'm going to be adorable.

My Panera boyfriend and I mostly discuss politics and contemplate the world situation, but we occasionally engage in playful banter and serious flirting. He might ask, "How about a little something, something?" My response would be, "Not in your wildest dreams." He's persistent, and I have fun managing his expectations.

Much of my writing is salty, humorous prose. He, more than anyone else, shows an interest in it. I read to him, and we laugh together. We spend just enough time together for Panera regulars to conclude we are a couple. That conclusion is impossible to dispute, so we declare our boyfriend/girlfriend connection without reservation. And I hold on to the illusion I've still got *it*, whatever *it* is.

I have a policy of not responding to his texts or phone messages, and we've had no contact outside of *my office*. Boundaries are required. I haven't had a date since the Dixie Chicks won best album ten years ago, and I'd rather stay home and watch crazy cat videos than go out to dinner. Our Panera connection is solid, though. The conversations are spicy enough to be described as near-sex experiences, but I firmly decline all propositions. There ain't no way in hell I'm going to touch that. I'm not that brave. When he suggests we ride off into the sunset on his motorcycle, I remind him I can't be spontaneous. I have prescriptions.

Around nine-thirty Don, a retired educator who pretends to be grumpy, comes in. In his mind, he has a reservation for a certain seat. I forewarn innocents who consider sitting there, "Elmer Fudd will arrive at any moment to claim his seat, and it will not be pretty if you are in it."

On Tuesdays at nine o'clock, my weekly coffee group, The Pillars of Sloth, arrive. Because there is so much need for socialization among retired folks, the Sloths evolved into a large, noisy group even more disruptive than the Democratic socialists. Another coffeeshop kicked us out for being too loud, which at our age is an honor we embrace with pride.

The group is tight. At the funeral for one of our members, front row seats were reserved for us. We wore straw hats because our friend who died always wore one, partially for protection from someone throwing food. He was one of four of us who started The Sloths, and we were shocked when the group grew to forty-some people. We weren't sure we liked the loss of our small, intimate group, but we didn't know of anyone we wanted to exclude. So we adjusted to the nuances of a large gathering.

I often write at my Panera office until the lunch crowd ambles in, at which time I leave with a substantial amount of work completed. I also meet writers I coach there. That is not my only writing place, though. I go to The Writers Colony in Eureka Springs, Arkansas, several times a year. My room, which overlooks a forest, has no television, phone, or radio. Jana, the Colony's cook, prepares dinner for writers, and we eat family style and commune each evening. Other than that, no one bothers anyone, and a number of introverted, solitary, pensive, and often eccentric literary enthusiasts reflect and create. It is not a fun place, but rather a peaceful, meditative one with no distractions. It is a place where stories shape themselves and spill impetuously onto pages of books to come.

Virginia Wolf would appreciate this place to write. In *A Room of Her Own,* she bravely suggested that women should have a place to write. This suggestion appears obvious today, but in her time, women had nothing, really, and her position as a writer in early England was a novelty. Today, women still struggle with a place of their own for different reasons—the demands of family and careers. So Wolf's suggestion still applies. For an older person, a place to write can provide a reason to hold on. *Please, Lord, don't take me now. I'm in the middle of a story.*

A place to write does not have to be lavish, or sophisticated, or particularly comfortable, or totally free of distractions. It can be a coffee shop, a park full of noisy children, or Jake and Elwood's Cafe in East Oatmeal, Oklahoma. It just needs to be a place beyond the bounds of everyday living. I have that at Panera, *my office,* my writing place—a place where I take communion with myself, explore my mind, and write into a void. When I travel, I miss my writing place. When I get home, Panera welcomes me back like a ramped-up dog whose owner has returned from getting the mail.

Not a Morning Person

Coffee, coffee, coffee
Coffee
Coffee, coffee,
Everyone shut up
Coffee

(Source: the Internet)

Chapter 21

Paraphernalia

Misjudgment Redeemed by Right-On Intuition

Georgetown is a happening place. I'd been there many times and assumed it a safe place to navigate alone, even at night. So I headed there by myself after an exhausting all-day business meeting near the Capitol. Still in my business suit, I would not be out of place. There were always politically-connected young professionals interspersed with locals, tourists, and college students.

It was dark, and I was hungry. Alone and unfamiliar with finer restaurants in the area, I came up with a failsafe strategy to find one. I'd target young professionals out for dinner before hitting the partying circuit and follow them to a nice restaurant.

The taxi driver dropped me off in the midst of a bustling crowd of diverse street walkers. Music wafted into the street from pubs and cafes. I soon spotted a group of sophisticated-looking young folks walking purposefully along the sidewalk, weaving their way through the burgeoning evening party crowd. One member of the group was obviously so stoned the others had to lead him around, but other than that, they appeared to be a cultured, well-financed, proper bunch. No doubt, they were pursuing an exceptional dining experience before hitting one of the trendy nightclubs. I tailed them.

When they turned a corner and headed down a side street, I speculated I'd be dining at an extraordinary, obscure restaurant. After walking some distance, the street lights became farther apart, pedestrians dwindled down to nothing, and the Potomac River shone like a tin roof through trees at the end of the dark street. The atmosphere took on a spooky quality, but confident I would soon be salivating over a luscious meal at company expense, I continued to follow.

This assumption disintegrated as I trailed the young folks through a grand door typical of places where one would expect to have a fine dining experience with Beluga Caviar and prancing grapes. What I discovered was a grand, flamboyant sexual paraphernalia shop. Definitely out of my element, a panic equivalent to finding an alligator in a swimming pool swept over me.

Whips and studded black leather items hung from walls. Display cases held perplexing mechanical devises and curious metal and rubber objects in all shapes and colors. A display of bras incapable of covering nipples bore a sign which said, "Cups of Love." Lacy garters and panties mingled on racks with Speedo-like men's underwear. Prominently displayed books with exotic covers and nasty words assaulted my mind, and blow-up dolls hung from the rafters.

The young people I had followed fanned out to examine the merchandise, seemingly comfortable with erotica. For me, the panic didn't come in a wave; it was more like a tsunami. I stood paralyzed except for eyes blinking and head spinning while trying to act like I meant to be there.

A tall, skinny, tatted-up young man with an outrageous purple Mohawk and a studded dog collar-like neck band approached. A black leather vest barely covered his smooth, oiled-up chest, which sported an impressive six-pack that struck me at about eye level. A studded belt with a shiny belt buckle styled like handcuffs was impossible to ignore. Tight, low-cut leather pants failed to hide troubling pubic hair and harbored a threatening bulge that was barely contained. Struggling to avoid engaging in an episode of serious crotch watching, my eyes darted around the store like a pinball seeking a place to land.

"Can I help you, ma'am?" the sex-toy aficionado asked.

I wanted to run—not walk—out the door. Instead I grappled with a way to maintain some semblance of dignity. The deer-in-the-headlights look on my face must have intrigued the young fellow. No doubt he enjoyed terrorizing me as he proudly suggested I consider the store's exceptional display of vibrators. "Of special interest is our popular throbbing rabbit model and the amazing flapping butterfly. Customers give them rave reviews." My mind grappled with absorbing the descriptions while my vagina went into lock-up mode and headed for my throat.

"Thank you," I said while pretending to be interested in a red negligee I pulled from a rack. When I noticed it had no crotch, I returned it.

"Our thigh-high, fishnet hose selections complement that nicely," he said. "They are available in black or red."

Go away. Please, please go away.

Finally he did, and I beelined it out the door.

After becoming a writer, I now occasionally put myself in awkward situations, which are out of character for me, solely for the prospect of a story. But I was not a writer at that time. In retrospect, I wish I had been more comfortable with the sex shop experience. It could have produced interesting fodder for a story. But the motive for this voyage was solely dinner at a fabulous restaurant. When contemplating why I didn't stay, out of curiosity if nothing else, I conclude it was the pubic hair that did me in. No amount of permissiveness could nudge me beyond the pubic hair. And so, I made my cowardly escape.

The hasty retreat seemed like a good idea at the time, but once outside, darkness and the remoteness of the location suggested otherwise. As I looked up the street to the lights of the bustling main street of Georgetown, I realized I had a substantial up-hill hike in heels to get there. After briefly considering re-entering the erotica store, I put the strap of my purse over my head and across my chest, got a serious grip on my briefcase, and took off.

I knew to walk with purpose and to display confidence. About halfway to my target, a spooky-looking man crossed the street and headed straight for me, his eyes focused on his prey. My intuition kicked in. I picked up my pace. He picked up his. When he lifted a finger and said something about needing directions, I was barely out of his reach. I took off running as fast as my high heels would carry me.

When I reached a bustling, well-lit street, I caught my breath and slowed my pace to match the rhythm of the crowd. *Did that just really happen?* I entered the first eatery I came across and had a hamburger and fries for dinner while blaring music and abrasive acoustics assaulted my ears. After that, I hailed a cab and got the hell out of Georgetown.

In the comfort of my hotel room, I ordered bread pudding and a glass of milk from room service and wondered about the motives of the man who advanced toward me with such aggression. Did I have a near-sex experience? Was he after a real sex experience. . .or my soul? Or did he want my purse? Maybe he was after my briefcase and the computer inside? Or perhaps he just wanted directions.

The Shakes

A frail, hunched-over elderly lady hobbled into a sexual paraphernalia shop, shaking profoundly.

"Can I help you?" the clerk asked.

"Yes. Do you have a pink dildo eight inches long, with a three inch circumference?"

"Yes, we do have that model. Would you like to see one?"

"Not really, but could you show me how to turn it off?"

Chapter 22

The Echo of Love

I couldn't dream that big.

Ron Mainer died twenty-some years ago. I've been thinking about him a lot lately. I do that when inching toward depression. His memory comforts me. Maybe he's on my mind because I'm going to die soon. I'm seventy-two. It could happen. I'm not ready. My five-year-old granddaughter, who had recently lost a grandpa, said to me one day as we cuddled on the sofa, "I hope you don't die soon, GoGo." I said, "So do I." There are no signs that outcome is imminent, but at seventy-something, the prospect crosses my mind from time to time.

I've wanted to write about Ron, about us, since I started writing eight ago. I never did because I knew doing so would produce an agonizing episode of painful mourning. I didn't feel up to such deep sentiment. I try to keep my emotions steady these days because I often feel fragile. Normal aging experiences do that to a person.

When we met at a singles event forty-some years ago, it surprised me he showed interest in me. Beat down from my marriage, I thought I was unlovable. We were both newly divorced and trying to find our way in a strange world.

The physical attraction between us was strong from the beginning. Ruggedly handsome, he was a country boy and outdoorsman. Years of sun exposure left him tanned and a tad leathery, which was attractive to this once-upon-a-time country girl. Lush hair, the envy of many a balding man, complemented shiny, sparkly eyes. An upright posture reflected hard-earned self-assuredness, and a lean, wiry build betrayed exceptional strength. Ron could be described as a "don't mess with me, buddy" kind of guy. Still, he had a silly side. Perhaps the most significant attraction for me was that his "way of being" in the world reminded me of my dad.

Ron's upbeat nature, strong persona, and absolute integrity were just what I needed after my divorce. He couldn't relate to my post-divorce depression. Depression puzzled him. He couldn't go there, yet he was compassionate toward those who did. A rough, tough, manly guy with a sweet sensitive side, he was, simply, a good man. Not perfect, but good.

If I had to describe Ron in one word, it would be real. There was no pretense about him, and he was a common-sense kind of guy. When I called him crying because I had a car accident, he asked if anyone was hurt. I said no. Then he asked if I had insurance. When I said yes, he said, "That's what insurance is for. You'll be fine." His counsel was always simple, to the point, and rich with practical advice. He advised people never to loan anyone money. Just give them some. He suggested to my kids that nothing good happens after midnight, and they proved his point several times over. He preached to never stay in a bar if there had been an argument or if someone had a gun. I learned his position on this issue one day while we were having a good time with friends. He suddenly got up, thew money on the table, and said, "Come on. We're leaving." In the bar parking lot, he grabbed my hand and urgently pulled me toward his car as he explained. "A man's jacket came open as he leaned over to shoot pool. He had a gun. Don't ever be in a bar with a man with a gun."

When we met, I fell hard and fast. Nervous about me becoming too serious, he broke up with me after six months. We both dated other people. He repeated a pattern of breaking up with women once things got serious. I was devastated and obsessed over him for about a year. Still, I carried on. This was a significant time in my life because disappointments in relationships taught me no white knight was going to rescue me. If I wanted something, I had to get it myself. This propelled me into a level of fierce independence that never faded, and it caused problems in relationships. I refused to depend on any man for anything. This attitude didn't make a man feel good. Although I dated others, I focused primarily on my career and developed a level of personal strength and fortitude I could not have imagined in earlier times.

During this time, Ron and I kept in touch and became confidants, even advising each other on relationships. He felt bad about his pattern of hurting women by breaking up with them for getting too serious. Finally, he decided to take a break from dating. I was unattached at the time, and we tried doing the friend thing. It didn't work. The passion flared again.

He was like a father to my son, Marty, at a critical time after the divorce when his father abandoned him. To this day, when we talk about Ronnie, Marty and I get teary-eyed, sort of like when we reminisce about Joey, a beloved family pet. Perhaps it is strange to relate feelings about Ron to those inspired by a bygone pet, but I'm a hard woman and few things bring me to tears. These two do so.

Ron taught Marty how to fight when we first moved to Tulsa. Junior high boys at his new school bullied him. "You're going to have to fight them," Ron said. Having grown up in a tough neighborhood as a hick country boy who moved to an urban area, Ron got beat up routinely until he realized the value of fighting back. "You will lose the fight," he said to Marty, "so your objective is not to win. It is to hurt the bullies so bad that they don't want to fight you again. Target the leader. Go in hard. Catch him by surprise. Take the first punch and hit, hit, hit. Put everything you've got into it. It may be the only chance you get to land a punch."

"But I'll get expelled for fighting," Marty said.

"It won't matter. Your Mother is talking about moving so she can get you into another school anyway. You've got nothing to lose. It has to stop one way or another." Reluctantly I endorsed the approach, and Ronnie taught him boxing techniques.

The next day the bullying began when one of the perpetrators reached over Marty's shoulder before class and snatched his pencil. Marty turned around and threw a powerful punch, hitting the guy squarely in the face. The force knocked him to the floor as his chair flew across the room. Marty braced himself for another agitator. There were no takers. He retrieved his pencil and sat down. The bully, stunned and red faced, recovered his chair, and sat rubbing his jaw. His cohorts were frozen in their seats. "Wows" and "Oh my gods" ping ponged around the room. Several people laughed.

The teacher wasn't present yet, and no one reported the altercation, so Marty didn't get suspended. The bullying stopped. Several boys in the room, who had experienced their share of intimidation from this fellow and his friends, befriended Marty. They are friends to this day.

Years later Ron taught Marty how to tie a tie for the prom, helped him buy his first car, and bailed him out of several teenage crises. He was a rescuer by nature.

At Ron's funeral the preacher said, "If you had Ron Mainer for a friend, you didn't need any other friends." And that was true. The minister pointed at the funeral audience and moved his arm slowly from one side of the room to the other and back again while he said, "Ron Mainer invested in almost everyone here, and YOU owe him a return on his investment." The room was dead quiet. Heads nodded.

A loyal devoted friend, he maintained relationships with those he went to high school with. One of them told me about the time he and his wife were on the expressway headed out of downtown in the early morning hours after a night of partying. When they spotted Ron's truck headed in the other direction, the guy's wife said, "That must be Ron headed to the jail to bail someone out." They learned later that's exactly what he was doing. Everyone's Huckleberry, Ron was the guy his friends called when they needed something.

Because of my fierce independence, I was hard to rescue, but Ron was generous with emotional support and sound advice. He always championed me and had my back. Our relationship was off and on for almost six years, although I would not describe it as rocky. I don't recall us ever having a fight, and harsh words were spoken only once, on my part. (I'll get to that later.) Although we broke up several times, the love was always there—undeniable, unconditional, unquestioned. Basic incompatibilities were what haunted us, driving a wedge into the connection.

Although Ron rarely drank at home, he sat at a bar for hours every weekday after work drinking and bantering with buddies, often until bedtime and without dinner. I joined him occasionally. He was a jolly drinker and at some point would turn into a mushy boyfriend full of sloppy I love you's. I'd have to beg him to feed me.

His first line of response was to order peanuts and pretzels. This became a joke among his friends, who volunteered to feed his woman. I knew I would prevail, and he'd take me out to eat. There wasn't much he wouldn't do for me. I am not much of a drinker, and a bar was not someplace I liked to be except for an occasional fun night out. This incompatibility complicated our relationship.

Although Ron enjoyed his drinking buddies, he rarely drank outside of their "clubhouse" bar and was functional and responsible in every aspect of his life. As a plant manager, he opened the plant every morning at six o'clock, never missing a day. My work ethic was strong as well, and our mutual respect for each other solid. He never complained about the demands of my career.

We were so in love that one summer when my kids went to stay with their grandparents for a month, we decided to live together, spending alternative weeks at his house and mine. This lasted less than a week. Ron didn't come to my house one night as scheduled. He called from the bar, apologizing sheepishly for not showing up, "You want to go home, don't you?" I asked. The line was silent for a moment, and then he said, "Yeah. I'm sorry."

"It's okay. Go home. I'll talk to you tomorrow."

I knew, and I suspect he did as well, marriage was not in the cards for us. We took full advantage of our month without the distraction of children, but never lived together.

I studied on weekends and late into many nights for the CPA exam and graduate school classes. In addition, I worked a demanding accounting job and parented two children. Exhausted, some mornings I cried when the alarm went off. I napped every chance I got. Ronnie never complained, but he knew I struggled to squeeze him into my schedule. I felt guilty about disappointing him. A high-energy, morning person, he never took a nap. When I slept in on weekends, he complained that I wasted the best part of the day. Another incompatibility. Eventually, the strain of our differences became too much, and we gave up.

We had one real fight. I reamed him out good. A woman where he worked had a crush on him. His work friends teased him about it, so I was aware of the situation. I didn't worry. I knew he wasn't interested, although I could tell he was flattered by the attention. How much was revealed at a company party where she zeroed in on him. He was tipsy and, as is common among men, had no idea he was being played or that his behavior humiliated me in front of our friends.

She kept his attention for most of the evening with her sparkling personality and charm, whispering in his ear, touching his arm, and generally being, in her mind, fascinating. She sucked him in. At one point she had him corralled on a sofa next to her. I went over and sat on the other side of him. He ignored me. She gave me that *ha ha* look women of her ilk give to other women. His attentiveness to her all evening was so obvious his friends noticed and felt sorry for me. One even offered to drive me home. I stayed and toughed it out. Ronnie paid the minute we got into the car to drive home. I went nuclear on him, delivering a rant extraordinaire followed by a cold shoulder that lasted all the way home. "I'm giving you to her as a present," I said as I slammed the car door and stomped up the driveway to my house.

The next morning he called, regretful and apologetic. He had no idea what he had done until I explained it to him. "She was the victor, I the victim. She fed your ego, and you took it in. The humiliation was complete." He got it. I forgave him and made it clear what I expected the next time he was around that woman in my presence. He was to pull me in close and say, "This is my lady. Ain't she great?" A couple of months later at another party, he did just that. I didn't give her a *ha ha* look. I didn't look at her at all. I just kissed him on the cheek and snuggled up, creating an awkward situation for her when he kissed me back, on the lips, long and hard. *My guy.*

Toward the end of our six-year, off-and-on relationship, Ronnie asked me to marry him. Pleaded, actually. This was a man in love. For once, I was the sensible one. I declined, not because I didn't love him and didn't want to marry him. I did. Oh, god, how I did. But I knew long-term the incompatibilities would chip away at us, and it wouldn't work. Also, my career was taking off, and my world becoming very different from his. The demands were all-consuming. I wasn't sure he could handle that.

"It wouldn't work long-term," I said. He didn't disagree with this conclusion but said he would take whatever time he could get. Wow. What a declaration. I remember vividly every detail about that conversation, where it happened, when it happened, his words, his demeanor, the pain in his face when reality closed in. I wanted to make him happy, to be with him, to live together for whatever time we could make it work, but I couldn't hurt him with what I knew to be the ultimate outcome.

Not long after that, we parted ways. It was painful for both of us. There were incidents of late night drunk dialing and accidental meetings that were not accidental. He called me late one night. I could tell he was hurting. I wanted to comfort him but was afraid of causing more hurt. I asked him what he needed and he said, "I just need to hold you." I wanted that, too. I drove to his house, and we embraced the minute I entered. As we stood in the entryway hugging, his body shook like a frightened puppy. The power of that moment, when this strong, vibrant man became so vulnerable he shook in my arms, is impossible to explain. I think of it often when I think of him, when I wonder what love is, when I feel dead inside.

It was a great love. For years after we broke up, we remained close until he got married. Even then, we met a couple of times after work for drinks. When I asked, "Ron, do you tell your wife we meet like this?"

He looked uncomfortable. "No." He was a man of integrity, and it was against his nature to be deceptive. We both knew in that moment what had to be done.

"You know we've got to stop meeting like this," I said.

"Yeah, I know."

We sat there quietly for a moment, awkwardly hunched over our drinks. Finally we looked at each other with tears in our eyes. That was the last time I saw him.

I sensed I would never love that way again, and I have not. I shook in the arms of another man years later as the reality of his rejection set in, but the intensity and vulnerability of that moment does not compare to holding Ronnie for the last time.

I could spend a lot of time on "what if's" and "if only's" when it comes to Ron Mainer, and I do sometimes. If I had known he was going to die when he did, I would have married him—tied my life to his and taken him in. But mostly, I push all thoughts of him away. I'm in my seventies now, and I don't know how much time I have left. I don't want to torture myself. I don't think I'll ever be able to think about him and not weep. I wish I could, but I can't.

Although Ron died some years ago and my vision of him has taken on the misty quality of a dream, the passion surrounding our connection is as intense as it ever were. Like an echo, these emotions come back to me when I allow myself to ponder the past. The feelings are deep and fierce. And they are real. I could never make them up because I could never dream that big.

The Tenacity of Love

The echo of love gingerly hugs
through seasons changing like wallpaper.
The architecture of love, cradled in memories,
shaped by time—gentle time—lives still.
Clunky, honest, eccentric, intoxicating love—
a merry blunder that never fades.
It was and is a great love.

Sweet, naked, and raw memories spiced with regret
swirl like smoke through my thoughts.
This love is not broken by the love of others,
not broken by the practicalities that fractured it,
not broken by time, not broken by death.
This love is nothing less than always.

Nestled in the fabric of two souls,
It is a forever love.

———————————————

There is a field. I will meet you there. . .Rumi

Chapter 23

The Impertinence of Aging

Statistically, I should be dead by now.

In a foul mood during line dancing class with fifty-some old folks, I contemplated leaving at the break. Then, I noticed a woman in a wheelchair wistfully watching the dancers. A sense of my ungratefulness slammed into me hard. I decided to stay. And the music seemed more vibrant, my dancer compadres more precious, and my world, at seventy-something, more remarkable.

Aging is a cruel master. I'm tempted to surrender to it, and sometimes I do. With each hit, I fight with a vengeance initially, but ultimately, I'm often forced to burrow into acceptance and focus on distractions. With the naïveté of a rookie, I take degradation in stride and settle into a state of coexistence wherein the zest for life ebbs and flows, but gratefulness flourishes.

When I turned seventy, three hits in a row reminded me of where I was headed. Bam! Bam! Bam! Diabetes, blood pressure fluctuations, and tendon and ligament damage from a prescription drug slowed my roll. I allowed myself to cocoon into a narrow and brief depression. I needed that to heal mentally and physically. But I knew I'd eventually recover my spunky self—if I didn't die.

* * *

As health issues invade, disconcerting waves of fear whisper in my ear and challenge my sense of gratefulness. In the past, medical crises surfaced and then transitioned into redemptions. Now, transient conditions leave permanent marks that cumulate into a collection of complaints. The battle has been mostly won to date, but I know where I'm headed. I'm a ticking time bomb, only as strong as my weakest part.

It doesn't help to believe everything happens for a reason, because I'm an off-the-charts, pragmatic realist. I hold the position things don't happen for a reason. Things happen. It's that simple. And I'm okay with that. I accept the logic of the universe and get more comfort from that than believing some spiritual being is so enthralled with my life that he is manipulating it.

What keeps me positive is knowing those who care about me want me to be okay—need me to be okay. If I can be okay to the end, no matter what happens, and let go gracefully of that which is no longer mine, I can soften their worlds and leave a grand and enduring legacy. Rather than complicating their lives with regrets, worries, and burdens, my intention is to own my third-trimester life experiences and do aging and dying well, even with the worst-case scenario—being in a nursing home with a room like a stall.

So, out of necessity I consider myself on the sweet side of seventy—a person in crescendo—even though this body is never summer ready, something weird is happening to my elbows, drugs are delivering nasty side effects, and statistics predict my ultimate point of demise. I relish every day, value every friend, and generously share my talents and wisdom. Unlike most writers who carry books in their trunks to sell, I carry them around to give away. If someone wants to throw money at me, I'll take it, but my primary goal is sharing.

I like to think that age is not the most important thing about me, but mostly it is. So, when I turned 69, I decided to be brave and face the inevitable head on. I threw myself a Pushing 70 birthday party to ease the trauma of transitioning into that dreaded seventy benchmark the next year. On my seventieth birthday the next year, I dolled up, put on a happy face and declared, "This is what seventy looks like. At seventy, I haven't even peaked yet." This was only a partial truth. Things were going downhill.

I took a test to determine my biological age, hoping it would be less than the chronological one. The results showed just the opposite. A family history of heart disease and a diagnosis of diabetes robbed me. Statistically, the average age of death for a woman in my condition is behind me. I'm consoled by the fact I've beaten the odds so far but, holy shit, I should be dead by now.

I wish I could say the body deteriorates but the mind does not, but that's not true. I wish I could say the wars of menopause are behind me and life is grand, but that's not entirely true, either. I wish I could say I'm okay with foreplay being replaced with floorplay (I fall down), but I'm not. I wish I could say that when the stock market tumbles I just watch, knowing it will rally eventually, but it is unlikely to do so in time for me. I wish the times I search for my car in a parking lot were not increasing, but they are. I wish I didn't have to fight for relevance, but I do. And I wish I had enough influence to convince my granddaughter that she does not need a boyfriend.

Then there are the regrets. I wish I had told one fellow that he would never be the man his mother was. I regret wanting to slap a pregnant woman who asked me where I got that cute maternity top when I was seventy. I regret allowing a man to install surround sound in my house. That would have been fine if Bonnie Raitt or Aretha Franklin blasted away, but I was forced to listen to Jimmy Hendrix and Def Leppard. If I hear Free Bird one more time on surround sound, I'll go insane. I regret I didn't give men more trouble in my younger years and that I gave them so much in the later ones.

I don't regret yelling, "Bail, damn it, bail!" to a bunch of drunks on a sinking boat or my plan to abandon them and jump off the opposite side in one of the few lifejackets if it sunk. There were not enough floating objects to go around, and I had children at home. I wasn't going to drown from some drunken fool pulling me under. And I don't regret the writings in an old journal rich with whining narrative. I was a victim then, flat out.

I don't regret getting high and eating the best carrots in the universe and believing I could pluck my eyebrows with a roach clip. And then there is this: Frankly, some men deserve to be called dickwads. There were occasions when being a bitch was required. Fortunately, I can also be a man's champion and the most generous, best badass friend he ever had.

When it comes to growing old, everyone is afraid on the inside. Sometimes it shows on the outside, and I cower like an abused dog. A precarious future promotes anxiety, but a history of bruised memories and thrilling highs are rich with lessons learned. When these are interpreted as assets, they become instruments for sharing wisdom. Doing so mitigates fear, inspires courage, engenders a sense of purpose, and propels me beyond aging well to aging in a way that makes a difference in the lives of others. I still have a lot to learn and to share, so I study my craft, expand my mind, and engage in advocating and sustaining. I know anything learned becomes a part of me. It is a possession no one can take away, except maybe the dementia fairy. I can't do anything about that so, well, fuck her very much.

My grandchildren lie on their backs in a tent and contemplate the disasters from which it protects them: bad guys, bombs, spewing lava. I have my own figurative tent: the premise that when something is lost, something else is gained. This is *almost* a universal truth. When I can't live in my house anymore, I won't have to deal with what home ownership entails. In senior housing, I'll never have to call a plumber or go through the frustrating process of seeking a rebate for the installation of a hot water heater.

Adjusting to losses these days is a circular process. I should not eat ice cream because of diabetes. So a nice distraction from the craving would be to go to a senior dance Friday night and have a boyfriend by Saturday morning. Or I could just eat ice cream.

I forage for cozy upsides to harsh downsides. If I had not lived to be seventy-one, I would have never had diabetes. There is an upside to everything. Two sisters I know who are losing their vision talk about giving each other makeovers when they can no longer see. Okay. Okay. That's a bad example. I don't apologize for it, though, and if you don't like it, you won't like the next one.

When in a wheelchair, I'll only have to iron the front of my dresses. I won't die untangling a vacuum cleaner cord, trying to get rust out of a toilet bowl, or scraping concrete out of a casserole dish. When I can't hear so well, I won't have to listen to ambient techno music in restaurants. When I can't see, I won't have to solve a technical quagmire, unfriend political fanatics on social media sites, or stay on my computer longer than I want to because someone is wrong on the

Internet. And, never again, will I have to say, "Well, aren't you the little rascal," to a help desk *child* who asks me if my cookies are activated.

I may not have big dreams, but I have short-term goals, things like converting a bong into a vase. Fitness will eventually take a back seat, but I can do chair yoga and claim I did a pushup when I actually fell down. I can learn Spanish from listening to Julio Iglesias songs. This may be as close to a near-sex experience as I get at that point. And when people talk about me and my situation like I'm not in the room, I can remind them I am, by god, a grown ass woman.

My plan is to look aging and dying square in the face. Peace is found in acceptance of the inevitable. Like Chief Tecumseh who said, "Die like a hero going home," my goal is to do dying well and to leave the world better because I was in it. I will go for a good goodbye. If I can deliver that, I will have done a good thing. I do wonder, though, if I died, would the manager of Village Inn miss me.

To the universe, I am prey, but I console myself with the fact that wrinkles don't hurt and I still have eyebrows. More importantly, I can still matter. I can make a difference. I can orchestrate my aging experience not as a burden to those I love, but as a gift. This requires constructing it within the confines of a cruel reality while polishing it up with blessings shared, gratefulness demonstrated, and considerable planning. Striking a bargain with life, I pledge that if I get it, I will live it full out. I may flounder now and then, but mostly, I will show off. Aging is, after all, the universe showing off.

Vintage with Game

I am a woman laced with contradictions—dancing duets
of oppositions.

I embrace my aging experience for I know growing old is a gift.
And I'm thankful for a long life not everyone gets.
So I use this time to create legacy because legacies are forever.
Still—reality is a severe and angry truth.
Tsunamis threaten and the gradual decline haunts.
Suddenly-one-moment incidents hover like angry poltergeists.
Not ready, it is as though aging is happening to someone else,
    and I am just a voyeur.

I am aging beyond well. This is my time.
These are encore years—better than the original show.
I celebrate life by cherishing the wisdom of experience
    and reveling in the fruits of my labor.
In the mirror, a magnificent being is reflected.
I admire the resilience etched in that deeply inhabited face.
On another day, though, I recoil from the same image.
Jolted by the revelation, I melt and wonder if I'm bipolar.

I am strong—at least somewhat and sometimes.
I ignore frailties and go all out until fate prevails.
Then, I pretend vigor. In private, I melt into feebleness.
Harsh truths reveal I am only as strong as my weakest part.
Physical vulnerabilities gnaw at my gut and prospects torture,
    for I know I am a ticking time bomb.
Recognizing that to the universe I am prey, I shake like a
    baby rabbit in a human hand.

Still, I am grateful. I'm still here. I'm still relevant. I still matter.
Happily, I soldier on as a woman laced with contradictions.

Chapter 24

Florida in *Carpe Diem* Mode

I didn't need to read the article on how to get a bikini body. I know how to do that. Put on a bikini. . . . A sassy old Florida woman

Wrestling with the airplane seatbelt, I complained, "It's just so-o-o-o mechanical." The most complicated device I ever mastered was a stapler. I left my home in Tulsa, Oklahoma, to meet up with Texas girlfriends, Aniston and Pepper, at the Houston airport. We were bound for Panama City Beach, Florida—a place known as The Redneck Riviera.

The three of us were going there to hook up with our friend Parker, also from Texas, for a girlfriend adventure.

This girl-trip had the potential to contrast sharply with my simple life as a writer, which is a mostly solitary profession. I was so devoted to my craft that friends had to drag me kicking and screaming from my computer to get me to do anything else. Since I took up writing after retirement, I had transitioned into an introverted and inert, but enthusiastic, author of miscellaneous rhetorical dribble. This meant a computer and WiFi were at the base of my hierarchy of needs. Aniston—a much younger sophisticate with a robust zest for life—was postured to liberate me from the humdrum of this profession.

As I settled into the obnoxiously uncomfortable airplane seat, I told her and Pepper, "I need this. My life has been too tranquil. I haven't even had a near-sex experience in ten years." The girls were, no doubt, surprised by this candid admission, but their laughter demonstrated an appreciation for the humor my dilemma provided, even though they could not relate to it.

I had left my computer, which normally served as an appendage, at home. This produced a constant, gnawing sense I had forgotten something—a feeling experienced years ago when I dispatched my children to grandparents every summer. I recovered quickly, though. Aniston, an effective distraction from anything that might interfere with the joys of the present, exuded energy and a gleefulness on the level of a hyped-up Pomeranian. Her influence was better than a B-12 shot.

A collector of fabulous people, she champions those in her circle as though she were their agent. Anyone needing an ego boost can get it from Aniston. Being with her is like curling up in a soft comforter and being yanked out occasionally to party. A lovely, strong woman with intense eyes, a luscious head of brunette hair, and a determined nature, she possessed a brave disposition, a nurturing maternal quality, and a knack for merrymaking. Because of her buoyant influences, I would be her wingman anytime.

On the plane, I met Pepper for the first time. A stunning elfin almost forty years my junior, Pepper exuded playful energy and a Bohemian hippie vibe. She possessed the moxie to wear petticoats under dainty sun dresses. With her delicate frame, fine features, and whimsical personality, she initially touched my motherly instincts. However, Pepper soon demonstrated she could hold her own as a woman of the world. A fearless, plucky babe not to be underestimated, her complex character could not easily be categorized. She rocked a streetwise quality and an audacious, worldly sense of adventure.

Before the plane took off, Aniston opened a sandwich bag filled with mini bottles of vodka and said, "Let's get this party started." Although I knew Grey Goose was gluten free and contained no sugar, the probability of a diabetic incident in my immediate future was disturbing. So I stuck to my protocol and abstained, demonstrating insipid common sense.

Experience had taught me people on vacation who start drinking in the morning often do not consider eating a priority.

This thought could have dampened the moment; however, as I contemplated how to find my niche in this tribe, I reminded myself Aniston appreciated me for all my flaws, edges, and uptight personal preferences. Since I valued the diversity of women of all ages and character and held sisterhood dear, I settled in and drew strength from anticipating a girls' adventure extraordinaire with a collection of fabulous Texas women fortunate enough to be included in Aniston's world.

* * *

The younger sister of an old boyfriend of mine, Aniston kept me years ago when her brother and I broke up. When she invited me to spend four days in Panama City, I hesitated to accept. A friend of hers, Parker, had rented a place there and invited friends to join her. Aniston and her gang are of my children's generation, and her inclination to invite a seventy-year-old woman on a girlfriend adventure was a mystery to me.

What were these girls thinking? Why would they include a woman who can't get into a hot tub because of blood pressure, who is saddled with a diabetic diet which excludes alcohol and consists mostly of kale, and who has a body that is never Florida ready? Relatively certain the girls had no clue what they were in for, I attributed their decision to naïveté.

This was not just about what they would think about me. It was deeper than that. It was about what I thought about myself. My own foolish inhibitions meant I excluded myself from potential life experiences. And I had not yet learned to love my tummy. Unlike many Florida women with an "aw, hell" attitude, I wasn't comfortable exposing my body with abandon—flaws be damned. Oh, the freedom of that. It must be exhilarating, but I could not get there. (Grandchildren would eventually nudge me in that direction, but not yet.) Instead, I wondered if Florida boutiques stocked longline swimsuits with sleeves.

So, in that unfortunate frame of mind, the need to protect the younger girls from themselves surfaced, and I considered declining the invitation. However, I had just finished a memoir in which I bragged shamelessly about how cool I was for an older woman. I even portrayed myself as a woman in crescendo, so it occurred to me if I didn't accept this invitation, I would be full of crap. So I decided to go and represent my generation, even though the experience was bound to illustrate the concept of "one of these things is not like the others." I hoped to inspire these younger women to not fear their own futures, which is what I'm all about these days.

To honor that perspective and as a matter of social reconstruction, I embraced the trip as an opportunity to demonstrate the robust life of a vibrant, fulfilled older woman, and hoped the others would not hold it against me that I was only marginally beach ready, could not eat ice cream, sip sweet drinks with umbrellas in them, or hold in my stomach.

* * *

So there I sat on an airplane with Aniston and Pepper while they got their buzz on. When we de-boarded in Panama City, they had no thoughts of lunch. Compelled by necessity to establish my diabetic protocol up-front, I grabbed a sandwich at the airport and ate half of it on the shuttle to Parker's place, hoarding the other half.

Immediately after arriving at the beach house, the girls faced the dilemma of deciding whether to pour Bailey's Salted Caramel or Bailey's Cherry Chocolate over coffee ice cubes. Those options plunged me into a world of discontent as I finished off the other half of my egg-salad sandwich.

At the beach house, I met our host, Parker, who didn't walk. She floated. Back straight, chin up, and legs moving almost in slow motion, Parker was so centered she gave off a regal vibe. When we entered her abode, she floated toward me and gave me a warm hug. I knew immediately there was something special about her—something powerful and contagious, yet subtle and contained. She exuded a sense of sharing as she observed her friends enjoying themselves. As I got to know her more, I concluded that being in the presence of Parker was like taking a Zoloft.

By renting the beach house for the season and inviting wave after wave of friends to enjoy it, she gave a generous gift. In a festive mood and reveling in our presence, she turned on music and danced around the room with abandon in a straw cowboy hat adorned with feathers, silver studs, and turquoise. With soft eyes, a deep tan, and luscious sun-bleached hair, she was a vision—"the bomb." It was easy to see why Aniston had collected her as a friend.

Parker was the kind of woman who loves rarely and breaks hard. On the tail end of a year-long, gypsy-like healing experience after the breakup of her marriage, any palpable pain had been eradicated. She had found peace, discovered the power of her essence, and was in the process of reinventing herself. Radiant, calm, and resplendent in her reclamation, she personified *the power of she*. Although I'm normally not inclined to steal someone else's shine, I wanted to be her.

Parker eventually floated down to the beach and directly into the ocean with her ducklings jostling for position in line behind her— me last because I had this ridiculous notion I could keep sand out of my tennis shoes. Soon, I got foxy, acknowledged the inevitable, and no longer cared if I got sand in my shoes. Later, I loosened up even more as we settled on the balcony for girl talk. The girls drank wine while I ate nuts from my travel bag for dinner. At about eleven o'clock, Aniston got the munchies, began knocking around in the kitchen, and whipped up a meal worthy of a tailgate party.

A hearty breakfast the next morning got us going, and we hit the resort boutiques with vigor. In a crowded parking lot, Parker showed us how to parallel park: you park some place else. This day was filled with classic girl activities and intense bonding which evolved, at one point, into Aniston "calling me out" about what she interpreted as my issues. This was motivated by her mission in life—to assure that every person who crosses her path realizes the best version of themselves.

In pursuit of this objective, she can be bold and candid. Picking at old scabs, she told me things about myself I didn't want to hear. I didn't hold that against her because she was well-intended and generally correct in her interpretations. She led me through an analysis of my issues—remnants of a haunting past that had camped in my memory for years. I discovered my heart was marred with old wounds, bleeding and clotting still. I had joined the club of those who love no more.

Her probing exposed a couple of unfortunate relationship experiences mixed together like slush in my mind. This combination prevented a realistic interpretation of each of them individually. It is not in Aniston's nature to hold anything back. Her intuitive approach to my remediation delved deeply into my past and bordered on a therapy session replete with a reality check and a comprehensive treatment plan. Sometimes when I profess to be okay, I need a person who has the courage to tell me I'm not. Although, in some respects, I was on my game at this point in my life—brave, strong, and full of moxie—I was still broken.

After the last breakup, I resigned myself to no more relationships or even dating for the rest of my life. I even made up rules to make certain friendships didn't cross over into the territory of romance. No man gets in my car. I never get in his. No man comes to my house. I don't go to his. And don't even try to get me to a movie or out to dinner. Resurrecting thoughts of love gone feral, I even contemplated a writing project: "Relationships I Wish I'd Never Had." But that would be a misrepresentation. They were wonderful. They just didn't end well, and part of that was my fault. I was an idiot, and it was my own failings that haunted me and kept the feelings raw and urgent.

Aniston was determined to shift my thinking to a more positive place. I took her impressions and advice to heart initially, but since she did not reward my receptiveness with money or a puppy, I eventually eased back into my comfort zone. There I clung to the cowardly defenses to which I had become hopelessly addicted, the hallmark of which was the conclusion I would never love again. I justified this with the idea my issues were real and hard earned, and I would keep them.

This didn't mean I was unhappy. Like a house wrapped in foliage, I was surrounded by the soft, gentle things in life. I had grandchildren who believed I was the toy fairy and; therefore, a frigging rock star. My grown children had turned out to be amazing people. And writing provided me with a retirement career so rewarding I never needed a vacation from it. These were huge distractions from internal turmoil. Like Steve Martin grabbing a lamp when leaving his home in *The Jerk* and pronouncing, "This is all I need," these blessings were my salvation and all I needed to be happy—at least, so I thought.

Aniston's input gnawed at me gently after the trip, causing me to take communion with myself. I finally acknowledged the inconvenient truth of my interpretations. As a result, I made some measure of emotional progress. At least I could finally talk about the pain and not feel it. My mood shifted to a place where instead of crying because a relationship was over, I smiled because it happened.

* * *

The final day of our vacation was splendid, in a touristy kind of way. In *carpe diem* mode, our agenda included bar hopping along the beach. We started in the morning. Few vacationers were out. When beach bunnies finally surfaced, Pepper said, "Yea! People." The sad, sorry thing about this was they were spring breakers—nearly naked, hungover, hyped-up children.

As the sun broke through dissipating clouds, we headed from the bars to the beach where we held court all day, fending off spring breakers who fancied our prime spot. While basking under an abundance of sunscreen on the few parts of my skin not covered, I spotted a young man strolling along the beach. A vision, he ambled past in a camouflage wife-beater t-shirt, Wrangler jeans wrinkled a bit at the top of his boots, sunglasses, and a cap with the bill frayed and curled down on the sides, the kind embraced by trendy country and western singers. He sauntered toward girls in skimpy bikinis, his guitar swinging loosely from his shoulder. This man had country music written all over him. The universe was strutting its stuff.

Something came over me. Completely out of character, I yelled. Yes, I did. I yelled. "Hey! Come over here." He stood there a moment—a vivid manifestation of redneck macho candy—looked at us and then back at the spring breakers. Wisely, he concluded hanging with festive older ladies would be more lucrative than the college crowd. And, of course, we ladies had the ultimate enticement weapon—our gorgeous Pepper dressed in a knockout beach dress and smoking a cigar.

As this vision of ruggedly handsome manliness strode through the sand toward us, exuding a sense of intention and a manly swagger, we girls stared in amazement. *Have I died and gone to heaven? Is it my birthday?* This gift reminded me of when a Coke bottle dropped from an airplane in Africa in the movie *The Gods Must Be Crazy*. A spellbound native decided he had to return it to the gods by dropping it off the edge of the earth. Except, we were not going to drop this guy off anywhere. When the universe gives you a gift, you take it.

The troubadour purposely strapped on his guitar, lit a cigarette, and dug a pick out of his pocket. Doing what he was born to do, he crooned a song he had written himself. The boy could sing. With the right amount of swagger and country twang spiced with lyrics about wanting to be used and abused, his manly appeal induced thoughts of raping and plundering and not necessarily in that order. The performance was gloriously, fabulously wicked. We girls whooped and hollered, yee-hawed, and clapped. I was beside myself. *Okay, that just happened.*

I asked him if he knew any Vern Gosdin or T.G. Sheppard songs. He responded, "You bet." So I dug in my purse for tip money to keep the performance going. *I know*

I've got a fifty in here somewhere. As it turned out, it was hours before I gave it to him. He hung with us all afternoon in spite of the enticement of a plethora of young oiled-up, beach-bunny bodies decorated with piercings, butterfly tattoos, and black painted toenails.

As his story unfolded, it became apparent this talented man possessed a delightful vagabond spirit with a bit of a tortured, hard-living past—a requirement for soulful country singers. As he tuned his guitar and contemplated his next performance, it was impossible to overlook the essence of this complicated, captivating man.

The day heated up, and he took off his hat and the camouflage wife-beater t-shirt. The act was tauntingly cruel, and caused me to make a valiant but unsuccessful effort to suck in my stomach. For me—an admirer of the country boy type— a man in a wife-beater t-shirt tuning a guitar with dirty fingernails and squinting from smoke circling up from a cigarette hanging precariously from the corner of his lips (I was raised in the Marlboro era) represented fantasy squared. I wanted to paint his toenails, wash his truck, and scrub the blood out of his shirt after a honky tonk-induced parking lot fight. The sensation these thoughts provoked was equivalent to sucking on an Ecstasy pacifier at a rave concert. My conservative nature slowed my roll, though. This was not a sustainable model.

I suspected the fellow was living on beer and catsup and had a cocaine philosophy of life. Flawed as he was, he would be a dream coming at any woman; however, no doubt, hell would be coming with him.

A fantasy bound to fade, the near-sex experience ended for all of us there on the beach hours later. We tipped our lovely, talented entertainer generously, after which he offered to give us our money back if he could come with us. This was tempting beyond belief, but we left him there wandering over to a cluster of spring breakers. He looked wistful as we walked away, but I knew without a doubt he was the kind of man who was everything a woman wanted and nothing she needed. Keeping him would have been like dancing on the deck of the Titanic. Common sense prevailed.

He was a gift, though. I had the same feeling about this experience that I had after scoring a good deal on a classic 1957 Thunderbird—a vehicle that defined me and made me feel cool and worthy of the top of the line.

We ladies were soon cruising the beach road in Parker's convertible with music blaring. Singing and dancing in our seats to eighties tunes, we presented a severe contrast to the bump and grind music of the younger set blasting from clubs along the street. No doubt we were a mystifying sight to spring breakers not accustomed to old ladies in hats. Aniston took selfies that made our faces look as though they were reflected in a spoon. Parker waved her hands in the air and drove with her knees. And I buried dreams of honky tonk heaven.

We finished off our last evening at a country bar where I two-stepped with myself while carrying a Diet Coke and pretending I was Parker, all centered and brave. I was so happy in those moments I could have married myself.

In the midst of pounding music loud enough to make sternums vibrate, Aniston managed to counsel a young financial genius who hated his job. No doubt she persuaded him to resign in order to realize his dream of not working there anymore. Pepper dazzled the guys. Parker floated.

The next morning, with Oklahoma calling me and Texas calling Aniston and Pepper, we walked down the Florida airport concourse to our gate. Aniston said, "Let's get this party started." And we did.

Cynthia Vanderpool

Chapter 25

A Woman in Crescendo

Discovering What You Were Born To Do

A tormented soul, my eyes were almost swollen shut from hours of sobbing. It was three o'clock in the morning. My brother, Kelly, listened to my woes and consoled me as best he could. A shocking betrayal and romantic breakup had devastated me. While wrestling with this emotional crisis for several months, I somehow managed to not miss a day of work, but I was barely hanging on.

This night, pent-up hurt and anger spewed from me like a high-pressure faucet I couldn't turn off. The emotional drain from months of hurting left me in a fragile state.

My secretary, Donna, whom I considered my wingman, had kept my daughter, Mel, who lived in California, apprised of my condition. Over twenty-some years of working together, Donna and I had rescued each other from several professional and personal calamities and had formed a strong bond. This was not a girlfriend relationship. It was more of a woman-to-woman connection. Her loyalty was solid.

With her and Mel teamed up, I had two determined, resourceful women in my court. They thought they conspired secretly to save me, but I knew they were on the phone every day discussing my status. I had no doubt but that any rescue tactics were jointly determined. Donna pulled the trigger one day and told Melanie, "You need to come home."

I had hardly eaten for months, and the rapid loss of weight drove my blood pressure down. Donna encouraged me to eat, scheduled lunch dates with friends, and poured supplements into my coffee. One day I ended up on the floor of my office because I knew if I didn't go down, I would pass out. She called the company nurse. The two of them became collaborators a month before when the nurse commented that I didn't look good. Donna confided in her, and they teamed up to nurture me as my health declined. Another supporter.

The nurse watched over me until I rallied, keeping the door closed to assure no one knew. Donna sat at her desk like normal and made certain no one discovered that her boss was prone on the floor of her office looking like a corpse in a coffin. Although my physical deterioration was obvious to everyone, she wisely determined it would not be good for the men to know the extent of my condition. A woman displaying weakness of any kind in corporate America was a career buster.

Although I tried desperately to hide my deteriorating condition, it was clear the men had noticed. I knew that when those who were never nice to me stopped attacking me over every little thing. Even with this demonstration of compassion, Donna and I knew some men would pounce if an opportunity was ripe for putting me in my place.

The President was not one of these men. He entered my office one day to ask me a business question. I must have looked pathetic because he stopped dead in his tracks and stared at me. "How can I help?" he asked. I pulled myself together and said, "Help me find a realtor."

"I'll be right back." He returned with the name of a realtor. I'm certain he told her to take care of me because she teamed up with Donna and went well beyond her real estate duties to support me through the sale of my house and a move. They made certain I was never alone at the house with my ex.

Girlfriends also rallied around with emotional support. I don't mean to belittle their contributions to my sanity, but it was the collaboration of Donna and Mel that kept me going at work and made certain my career was not jeopardized by my madness.

To Mel, the vulnerability of her normally strong, in-command Mother was of intense concern. She had never seen me like this. It was hard on her. She wanted to come to Tulsa, but her company was going public and she had to be at the New York Stock Exchange when Donna decided it was time for her to come. I suspect Mel knew I would never forgive myself if my weakness caused her to miss such a life event. A resourceful woman, her solution was to enlist my brother, Kelly, who lived in Kansas City, to stay with me until she could get here.

When he arrived, I told him the details of what happened. A sensitive, rational, common sense kind of guy, his presence was a comfort that cuddled me like a soft blanket. The extent of the betrayal I had experienced shocked him. He gave good counsel but mostly just listened as pent-up hurt and anger spewed forth. I needed to vent, and I did.

By three o'clock in the morning, my eyes were almost swollen shut from hours of crying. Through all the trauma of the loss of my partner, I had managed not to miss a day of work. But that night, I looked up at Kelly through red, puffy eyes and asked, "I can't go to work today, can I?"

"No. You should call in sick. And it wouldn't be a lie. You are in no condition to work."

"I am sick. My gut hurts. I feel awful. I feel fragile, like I might break. And I feel so incredibly drained."

"You're tired. Let's turn in."

I surrendered to reality and agreed, although I loathed this concession to my delicate physical and mental state. It signaled failure, weakness, and shame. I had fought hard to keep the crisis out of the work environment, and now I had failed. My career was important, and work medicine—the only effective distraction from my personal struggle. This encroachment into the work part of my life was hard to take. But there was no denying it. I was done, defeated. Resigned, I accepted the inevitable.

The weariness I'd been refusing to acknowledge for months swept over me. A sense of release settled in as I headed to the bedroom and the escape of sleep. Then my memory betrayed my release. I recalled an important meeting scheduled for that morning. The prospect of a healing day of rest evaporated.

Turning to my brother, I said, "I can't stay home. I'm scheduled to train fifty-some customer service reps at seven in the morning before they go on the phones at eight. They are all coming in early for the class. It's too late to cancel. I have to be there. I can't standup all those employees. No way." Kelly knew I was right. We both possessed a strong sense of responsibility drilled into us by our mother. I would go to work. No exploration of options was even considered. We switched our focus from healing to strategizing.

"You can't go to sleep now," he said. "It's almost four. It'll be too hard to get up, and your eyes will swell shut. You need to stay up."

I agreed.

"And we've got to get those swollen eyes down." He made ice packs. I brewed coffee.

"I'll drive you to work," he said, sensing that even driving was too much for me.

I took a shower, washed and styled my hair, and put on layers of concealer. The activity was exhausting, but it distracted me from more crying.

*　*　*

At six o'clock I called, Donna.

"What do you need?" she asked.

"Set up a podium and a stool in the training room. I'll need to sit down. And get a microphone. My voice is shaky. Meet me at the back door with coffee—black. Kelly will drop me off. Be prepared to distribute the handouts. I'm not sure I can. And, Donna, plan to stay with me throughout." That was already a given. She would not leave me.

Donna met me at the door. I sat on the stool drinking coffee and trying to act normal while welcoming trainees and participating in normal morning banter. I was a mess. It was a "fake it till you make it" situation.

A strange thing happened as the training progressed. My voice got stronger, and my strength came back. I abandoned the podium and walked about the room and up and down the aisles as I always did when speaking. *I've got this*. Enthusiasm took over, and I did this for an hour. It was as though my normal, high-energy self could not be contained.

When it was over, I sat down on the stool, spent. After everyone left, Donna guided me to a cot in the company's medical office. I fell asleep immediately, waking briefly to take note of her covering me with a blanket.

* * *

In a therapy session a few days later, my counsellor listened to a litany of woes and then asked me to tell her something good about my week. I told her about that day at work. She lit up. "Do you have any idea what this means?" I didn't.

She explained, "This may be a hokey way of describing it, but it's possible you have discovered what you were born to do. It took you over and carried you through. Clearly you have an innate ability to teach. Otherwise, that wouldn't have happened." She was right, and her observation fostered a defining moment that influences me to this day.

My enthusiasm for training was driven by an innate ability straining to be expressed. When my counsellor articulated that, I "got it" immediately. Teaching was what I was born to do. It poured out of me. There was no holding it back.

Driving home from the counseling session, I recalled the day the corporate manager of training called to cancel a corporate supervisor training class I was scheduled to conduct because there were only three people signed up. Knowing the information I gave each participant in the class would affect over sixty employees and hundreds of customers every day, I insisted on doing the class anyway. The synergy of those results made the investment of my time worthwhile. It would most likely be the most important thing I did all week.

I had always considered training a priority. Investing in employee learning delivered huge payoffs. I not only trained my people, I volunteered often to train for the entire company. Other executives showed little interest in training and were quick to let someone else do it.

I wanted employees to know everything I knew. I kept a list of things I knew and learned and passed that information on in monthly management training meetings. I invited others to share what they learned as well. The sessions were so fruitful and popular employees from other departments attended. In addition, I trained on all levels. Each employee in my division had a personal learning plan every year.

As a result of my counsellor's revelation, I became even more of a teaching machine. And as an author after retirement, I taught writing. To teach, one must be in a state of continuous learning. So I took college courses on writing, attended writer conferences and workshops, joined writers groups, entered writing contests, participated in critique groups, and studied the experts. I studied the printing and publishing industry and formed my own publishing company. Soon I was speaking at writers' conferences, conducting workshops, and coaching novice writers. I even published "how to" books on writing and publishing.

* * *

Like the marrow in bones, a person's talent is set before they are born. Sadly, many people never discover what they were born to do. Some stumble onto it, but don't recognize the potential it offers. When I meet people, especially older people, I notice whether they are aware of their innate abilities. Those with that awareness live enriched lives because then, and only then, does the magic unfold.

This being said, it is important people not compare aptitudes. It is easy to conclude one talent is more important or more impressive than another. Some are flashy. Some are subtle. All are important. I teach my students: *Don't let anyone else's grand passion make yours seem small.* Never let what anyone else is or does rob jewels from your crown. Winning is not a victory over others, but over some other thing. It involves an improvement in self. Bette Midler would call it "a boob job for the soul." Do your own thing. Shine from where you are. And remember this: Just by being, you are enough. (And there I go ... teaching again.)

No one is ever too old to discover what they were born to do. Many a person has discovered new ways to be productive in their nineties. I'm in my seventies now. I continue to teach writing, and I conduct seminars for a university's continuous learning program on how to go "beyond" aging well. I rarely charge for anything I do. It is not about money. It is about sharing.

The key to this level of purposefulness is self-awareness. This requires a person be authentic and discover their own personal capabilities, which can be challenging. Consider those singers on the *American Idol* tryouts who are awful and yet convinced they have a wonderful voice. How can they be so unaware? Most likely, someone influential in their lives told them they could sing. That someone probably also said they could be whatever they wanted to be. Then, the judges tell them they can't. J.Lo calls them "baby" and says she's sorry. Keith Urban is tender with his "no." Harry suggests their talent doesn't lie in singing and encourages them to find their niche in something else. In the early days of *Idol*, Simon Cowell told them, "That was awful. Get Out."

Afterward, these contestants leave the tryout room and fall into the arms of loved ones who continue to encourage them to sing. As a result, many of these aspiring singers soldier on. What would their lives be like if their advisors had suggested they focus on discovering and tapping into innate capabilities—what they were born to do?

Aspiration, driven by external stimuli, obstructs the view of each person's unique talents and essential needs. When a person celebrates fads and idolizes the glamorous paths of others, their ability to realize their natural capabilities is inhibited. They cannot shape a realistic dream. Because of the influence of external factors—especially popular, flamboyant ones—viable options are obscured, and success trampled.

I've learned to never tell anyone, especially young people, "You can do whatever you want to do." That thinking sets them up for frustration and possible failure. Instead, I encourage self-discovery, "Find what you were born to do and do that." Everyone's innate talents are specific to them, kind of like a fingerprint. The way to realize one's potential is to discover inborn talent, develop it, and share it with others. Doing so will flow easily. It will light the person up because it is in their bones.

Discovering my innate talent changed the third-trimester of my life. I found my niche, a crazy wonderful place that fuels my energy, defines my purpose, and releases my talent. It emboldens, keeps me focused, and overcomes paralyzing self-doubt. It gives me a reason to keep going. It gives me game. With that powerful motivation, there is no coasting here. Even in my seventies, I am a woman in crescendo.

I've Got Game

I am relevant. I make a difference.
I seek enlightenment through continuous learning.
Wisdom emboldens, and I generously share it.
Opportunities to coast are resisted. Purposefulness prevails.
The intention is to matter—and I do.
I mourn my youth, but the advantages of age are relished.
I aspire to be a beacon in the eyes of the young.

I have a zest for life.
Reveling in the tenuous now, I ignore the precarious future,
At least as much as is possible. A pervasive uneasiness smolders.
Ghost-like, it torments with the terror of something grave.
I dream of it—a cloud that nudges me awake at night.
As coffee soothes, a gnawing anxiety dissipates.
The medicine is knowing I am enough. Just by being, I am enough.

Colliding with aging stereotypes, I rage, reframe, and evolve.
This is my time—my best time—and I am vintage with game.
Yeah, that's it. I've got game.
Naaah, I don't. Not really.
Yes, I do. I do. I really do. No, I don't. Yes. No. Yes.
Age is a persistent intruder, but my life is flush with purpose.
I am a mighty woman. I have game.

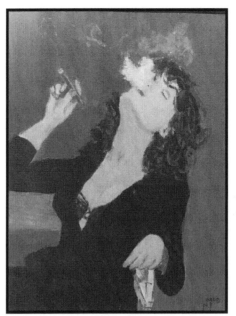

Painting by Nan McDowell

Chapter 26

Seriously?

*The purpose of life is not to be happy. It is to be useful and honorable, to be passionate, to make a difference by having lived and loved well."...*Ralph Waldo Emerson

An Oklahoma earthquake, one of many since fracking began, shook the house. It was a big one that rattled dishes and knocked a picture off the wall. I stopped, paralyzed for a moment, and then my irreverent tendencies kicked in. I got my freak on and interpreted the quake as the earth having an orgasm, which meant fracking was foreplay. I was jealous. This could be as close to a sexual experience as I was going to get, and I should celebrate by smoking a cigarette—or a cigar.

This fanciful interpretation of an earthquake illustrates a tendency to let thoughts get away from me. It is also an example of the power of envy. Everyone is barraged by temptations perfectly calibrated to create the *I wants*. By interpreting life through an external filter, people lose their way in a messy world of discontent.

A little girl announced to her mother, "I need a boyfriend."

"No, honey, you don't need a boyfriend."

"Yes, I do. I really do." Her face squished up into that misery and woe look children do so well.

"Why do you think you need a boyfriend?"

"Because my best friend has one."

"Trust me, dear. In First Grade you don't need a boyfriend. Someday you'll understand."

Desperate, she pleaded, "But I do. I really, really do."

"I'm telling you, you don't need a boyfriend. Trust me."

Close to tears now, frustration took over. "Please, Mommie, I need a boyfriend. Please. Please. Please. Will you get me one?"

The *I wants* can fuel discontent so intense it drives a person to take impulsive actions. A person might seek out island life only to find they are living among marauding monkeys, lizards, sand fleas, beach mites, bugs the size of shoes, constant wind, and humidity on the scale of a sauna. This is okay if you actually like that kind of thing and are not sucked into it by a glamorous TV program that portrays the preferences of others. When the *I wants* is driven by external rather than internal factors, distractions invade and desired outcomes flow uneasily.

Young people are driven to aspire to being famous because their idols are. Young girls want to be J.Lo and young men a rap star. Goals inconsistent with inborn talents distract from finding one's own unique passions. Before a person is born, their place in the universe is set. With no awareness of natural abilities, failure is inevitable, and failure creates victims. As victims, people take on faux crosses (burdens in their heads), and they carry them with intention.

Admiring someone is a good thing when the result is inspirational and leads to positive, personal outcomes. But advertisers, reality shows, and social media venues encourage comparisons that cause people to be dissatisfied with themselves and to not value their inherent qualities.

Another problem is that people often compare themselves to those in different age groups. When I was a corporate executive in my forties and fifties, young women just starting careers would compare themselves to me. They'd say something like, "I can never do what you do." I couldn't do those things either when I was in my twenties. And the thing is, these girls had a head start on me. When I was their age, I had no college education, my husband was not supportive, and my career was babysitting men as a secretary. These younger women already had degrees and had started professional careers. In their forties, they'll do what I did and then some. On the other hand, if I were to compare myself to these lovely, accomplished young women, I would not have fared well. I didn't allow their youthful advantages to influence my self-esteem, and I was never resentful of their head start. I was happy for them. *Good for you. You go, girl.*

* * *

For older people, it is often not the enticement of a fad or a popular trend (the *I wants*) that prevents them from capitalizing on their assets. Rather, traditions and societal expectations strangle them, preventing discovery of fresh, unconventional pathways to a life that is their kind of crazy wonderful. It is never too late to do that.

Young people are less constrained by traditions. They value the concept but are willing to tinker with requirements. My grandchildren, eager to do Halloween decorating in September, wadded up a piece of notebook paper and put it between the sheets in their parents' bed. The message, written in ominous bold, black letters, clearly defined their grievance: "Get the Halloween decorations out now, OR ELSE." Refusing to be restrained by tradition, they rebelled.

One thing children and adults have in common is that they are both quick to feel abused or deprived. As a child, I thought having four brothers was a burden. Then, a girl in my school who was an only child confessed she was jealous of me because I had brothers. I had always envied her, a popular girl who had two pairs of school shoes. Until that day, I viewed my brothers as animals who brandished a brutal sense of entitlement as they robbed, plundered, and pulled heads off dolls.

How much time do we waste wishing something were different from what it is? How many blessings are overlooked while we covet some shiny thing someone else has? How often are we enticed by external influences when we should be looking inside for what makes us happy?

Love comes from inside. If sought in earnest, love is possible. It should be embraced gingerly, though, because it is a brazen and fallible business. Plagued with hazardous undertakings, it is capable of delivering searing, unrelenting pain and the kind of grief that touches places a person didn't know they had. (I'm not bitter.) It is the summit of emotions, though, a deep stirring of the heart. A need. A desire. A gift like no other.

I've felt love, seen it come and go. I've rolled in it, melted into it, and swiped it off. I've valued it and cursed it. Still, I know nothing about it really, except it exists. Sometimes it is requited, sometimes not. Sometimes it is forever, sometimes not. There are no words to adequately describe or explain its pattern or its power, except to say it can go so deep it sweeps a person away.

How does one cope with love when it doesn't deliver? I used to hate the statement *It is what it is*. I interpreted it as trite and condescending, insulting even. But as I age and adjust to the unavoidable, degrading incidents that challenge my sanity, I've come to appreciate these words as a coping strategy. The value is in their proclamation of acceptance. And, when it comes to love issues, acceptance is the key to peace of mind.

As an expression of romantic love, sex is central. The problem is that sexual encounters transition from the robust nature of younger years to the near-sex experiences of older ones. It's tempting to allow nostalgia to interfere with the present. For those older folks who haven't had sex since *Fargo* won the Critic's Choice Award, desperate measures are often sought to kick-start the body, most of them complicated and risky, if not downright futile. *It is what it is.*

There is an alternative. We older folks can meet nature where it is and acknowledge that when something is lost, something else is gained. We can celebrate the natural order of things and chill in the soft mellowness of the now. We can appreciate whatever our worn bodies and seasoned minds have to offer instead of feeling disenfranchised. An elderly lady can accept arms that look like swim floaties and thighs the texture of cottage cheese. An old fellow can name a body part a dangling participle. . .Okay, that's just wrong. I apologize for the old people jokes. My thoughts got away from me.

Seriously, though, we can acknowledge the inconvenient truths of aging and avoid sinking into a state of malcontent. Instead, we can celebrate what vibrant, brilliant, robust qualities we still possess even though we might drive all day with a turn signal on, drive into the wrong end of a car wash, or scrape the sides of our cars on garage doors. We can exchange mis-matched socks for another pair of mis-matched socks and not feel inadequate. We can deal with aches and pains and celebrate that our earlobes don't hurt. We can avoid interpreting a new varicose vein as equivalent to discovering a raccoon in the attic. . .Sorry about those random, whacked-out thoughts. They're weird. Let's try something else.

A woman can appreciate she is recovering nicely from knee surgery rather than lamenting over the cause—her Great Dane, Knuckles, attempting to mount her as she bent over to weed a flowerbed. . .Wh-o-a! I apologize. That was a tasteless, crude example of oversharing. I lost my compass.

Seriously, why is it so hard to take communion with one's self, conclude the body and mind are in a natural state, and interpret that as a soft place to land? . . .Ugh. That's trite, and it incorporates a cliché, no less. Here is a more literary example.

Why can't growing old be like flies getting tangled in your hair as opposed to landing on the peach cobbler? . . .Forgive me. That simile got away from me. Neither option is good, and this example is definitely not literary. Let me try a different one.

Why can't growing old be like butter melting on toast? . . .Not so bad, though a tad hokey. It might have been more authentic and representative of the situation if the bread were moldy. . .Holy crap. Did I just compare being old to being moldy? I am s-o-o s-o-r-r-y.

How about this? Why is growing old like climbing a cactus?. . . I apologize. That's disturbing.

I give up. Being old *is what it is.* Seriously.

Love—A Powerful Temptress

I relish the fellows, but I am no longer a woman who sees
an attractive man and stands taller and reins in her stomach.

Prospects are murdered lest something inside of me breaks again.
Hugs are harvested, which comfort but do not complete.

Though yearning persists, I don't have another breakup in me.
A void intrudes, but that's okay. I fill it with writing,
teaching, grandchildren, and chocolate.

BOOKS BY NIKKI HANNA
Available on Amazon, Kindle, and www.nikkihanna.com

OUT OF IOWA INTO OKLAHOMA
You Can Take the Girl Out of Iowa, but
You Can't Take the Iowa Out of the Girl

CAPTURE LIFE - WRITE A MEMOIR
Create a Life Story—Leave a Legacy

WRITE WHATEVER THE HELL YOU WANT
Finding Joy and Purpose in Writing

RED HEELS AND SMOKIN'
How I Got My Moxie Back

NEAR SEX EXPERIENCES
A Woman in Crescendo, Aging with Bravado

HEY, KIDS, WATCH THIS
Go BEYOND Aging Well

LEADERSHIP SAVVY
How to Become a Stand-Out Leader, Promote Employee
Loyalty, and Build an Energized Workforce

LISTEN UP, WRITER
How Not to Write Like an Amateur—The Path to Authorship

AUDACIOUS
2016-2020—Five Years of a Special Kind of Stupid

WORKSHOPS AND PRESENTATIONS

LISTEN UP, WRITER
A Series on How NOT to Write Like an Amateur

Find Joy and Purpose in Writing—encourages writers to take a fresh look at why they write and to develop a definition of success that taps into innate talents and that is achievable.

Tap into Craft—The Road to Authorship—reveals common craft mistakes writers make—the ones that shout *amateur.*

Get the Most Out of Revision, Editing, and Proofing—ensures a writer produces work that is impressive enough to compete in the writing marketplace.

Nail the Structure—Beginnings, Endings, and In Between—covers how to write compelling beginnings and endings and how to keep the middle from slumping.

Write with Voice, Style, and Humor—shows writers how to find personal voice and style so their writing stands out from other writers, delights readers, and impresses publishers.

Capture Life through Memoir—Writing the Hard Stuff—shows how to write a captivating life story, how to write about difficult times and flawed characters, how to decide what to put in and what to leave out, and how to print and publish.

Create Compelling Nonfiction—covers writing principles that apply to various categories of nonfiction (biography/memoir, instructional, self-help, essay, inspirational, illustrative). Writing tips that apply to other genres and publishing options are included.

Apply Winning Strategies to Writing Contests—demonstrates how to be more competitive in contests and how to strategically select them. Key tips increase the odds of winning.

Evaluate Printing, Publishing, and Marketing Options—discloses nuances of the industry and describes the pros and cons of various publishing strategies so writers can make sound, informed decisions.

neqhanna@sbcglobal.net - www.nikkihanna.com

248

ABOUT THE AUTHOR

When asked to describe herself in one sentence, Nikki Hanna said, "I'm a metropolitan gal who never quite reached the level of refinement and sophistication that label implies." The contradictions reflected in this description are the basis for much of her humorous prose. She describes her writing as irreverent and quirky with strong messages.

As an author, writing coach, and writing contest judge, Hanna is dedicated to inspiring others. She speaks on writing and offers writing workshops on the craft of writing, memoir writing, writing contest strategy, writing with voice/style/humor, finding joy and purpose in writing, and other writing topics. She also speaks on aging, leadership, and women's issues.

In addition to numerous awards for poetry, essays, books, and short stories, Hanna received the Oklahoma Writers' Federation's *Crème de la Crème* Award and Rose State College's Outstanding Writer Award. As a self-published writer, her book awards include the National Indie Excellence Award, the USA Best Book Finalist Award, two international Book Excellence Awards, four Independent Book Awards, and an IPPY (Independent Publisher Book Awards). Her books are available on Amazon and through her website.

Hanna has a BS Degree in Business Education and Journalism and an MBA from The University of Tulsa. A retired CPA and Toastmaster, her years of experience in management and as an executive for one of the country's largest companies fostered a firm grip on leadership. She also served as a consultant on national industry task forces, as a board member for corporations, and as an advisor on curriculum development and strategic planning for educational institutions and charity organizations.

Hanna lives in Tulsa, Oklahoma. Her children decided she had become a bit of a pistol in her old age after she and her sixty-something friends were banned from a sushi bar for a food fight. They tell her, "Don't call me if you get thrown in jail." Four grandchildren consider her the toy fairy, and those in California believe she lives at the airport.

neqhanna@sbcglobal.net
www.nikkihanna.com